NEW LIFE

NEW DIRECTIONS

Registrants in Reentry

Bob Van Domelen

Paperback ISBN 978-1-957497-82-2

I dedicate this humble effort to my victims and for all victims, that each day for them is a new day, a day without fear, and a day of healing.

Contents

Introduction

For most individuals living in confinement, they know that eventually their world of prison life will come to an end. For many men and women nearing a release, there is an excitement that is hard to describe without sounding overly dramatic. For a few, however, that excitement might be replaced with fear or, at the very least, uncertainty mixed with anxiety. In both situations, outside of the barred and razor-wired environment they call home lay a world that had changed greatly since they last lived in it.

In 1989, I attended support group meetings for individuals offered by a ministry called Broken Yoke Ministries. The following year, the director of the ministry learned he would be moving because of a new job. After some discussion, he agreed to turn the ministry over to me rather than shut it down.

I got directly involved in prison ministry in 1992 after a workshop I led at Point Loma Nazarene College in San Diego. The talk I had given had gone well, and all that was left was to answer any questions raised by the audience.

A woman sitting near the front raised her hand. "In your testimony, there are three years missing from the timeline you offered. Can you tell us about that?"

I paused in a room that had suddenly grown quiet.

When preparing my workshop, I had figured no one would notice the gap, yet I had wondered if I should say anything. I knew, however, that if I answered the woman's question, things wouldn't be the same for me. Everyone in the room would know, and if they knew, how long before I might no longer be invited to do workshops.

Feeling a strange sense of calm, I took a deep breath and said,

Introduction

"During those three years, I was in prison for molesting boys. I still have shame and guilt for the things I have done, but I know that if my life is to change, I must trust God. Today, right now, I think, is one of those trusting moments."

There were no more questions, no "Praise God!" or "You aren't welcome here." Just silence. I later learned that my disclosure was widely discussed.

That conference was the beginning and a door-opening for what I have been doing every day since – corresponding with registrants (persons registered as sex offenders), writing a newsletter, publishing a book, and leading workshops where the topic is hope and encouragement for those society would rather have disappear.

My first book, *Can I Tell You Something* (Covenant Books), is shared among inmates in prisons around the country. The book was a series of reprints of articles I had written for *Into the Light*, a bimonthly newsletter I produce for those in confinement for sex-related charges and those who seek to support them.

Lately, some readers of the newsletter and my book have written to request a second book that addresses issues they might face in reentry. This book, *New Life - New Directions*, is meant to provide some of that information. The book won't satisfy every issue you might have, but I hope some of the suggestions I offer will make things easier for you.

I have also invited registrants currently in reentry (those with sex-related offenses) to share their experiences on various topics. Again, this book is more of a conversation I am having with you than a one-stop resource guide. But God willing, together we can eliminate some of the anxiety.

Finally, everything I write has a Christian foundation, though those who contact Broken Yoke Ministries come from a range of faith backgrounds or no faith background. It is my faith that has brought me to this point, so although I use a non-denominational approach in what I share with you, my basic belief is that the God who loves me loves all. He loves you!

Introduction

Throughout the book, you will find sections titled *In Our Opinion* (comments from registrants) and *Something to Ponder* (articles previously written for *Into the Light*) (ITL). Read both or skip until later.

The *Into the Light* articles have some focus with the topic of a given section, but mostly I included them as moments for thinking about the stuff that might be going through your mind as you deal with the day-to-day matters connected with reentry.

Some of the comments shared by those in reentry might not sound positive or could seem questionable, but they represent what these registrants feel based on their experiences, not on some success formula. My goal is not to correct what they share because the words represent how *they* feel. Reentry is the real world with ups and downs – the up times are great; the down times require a willingness to plow through them when they happen. You'll make it. Just hang in there.

Part One
Nearing the End of Inside

1

Change and Anxiety

In Wisconsin, confinement security levels are decided by one's sentence structure, but essentially prisons are set up as maximum, medium, and minimum security, based on the severity of the crime and the point system used for institutional placement. For most, the closer one is to a minimum level, the closer they are to being released. At least that's the general idea, because the pattern is not the same for everyone, but it's the pattern I experienced.

The judge gave me a 5-year prison sentence followed by a 10-year parole, so my institutional journey began in early 1986 at a medium security level institution. Though somewhat unusual, I was only there for a few months.

A new sex offender treatment program was being created at one of the minimum-security prisons. After an interview with the director of the program, he hesitantly decided I might fit in. His one concern was that I talked about God a lot, something he felt did not fit his program.

Along with a small box of belongings, I was transferred a few weeks later to Oakhill Correctional Institution near Madison, WI.

The program, while not easy, had the desired effect of getting me to consider what I had done, whom I had harmed, and the distorted thinking that made possible what should have been unthinkable.

While the program was secular in nature, the group facilitator didn't demand that I set aside expressions of the faith that guided my journey. If anything, he knew my faith in God demanded honesty and accountability as well as a willingness to challenge my dark side. To the best of my ability, I did and continue to do so. I think he knew that.

A Moment of Identity Anxiety

At the invitation of the institution's recreation director, I got involved with a few other guys singing some old standards. It wasn't that the music was so great or that we were such good singers, but we had been given permission to put on a program for the residents of the nearby state mental institution. I know. "How can you miss with a captive audience?" but we understood a little about confinement and wanted to do this. The program went as well as could be expected, and they clapped. Clapping is always a good thing for a performer.

As a bonus for helping, the warden agreed to let us stop at a low-end restaurant (not a fast-food place) on our way back to the institution. It was understood that we had to pay for our food choices, but the bottom line for us was that this was not prison food. This was "real people" food.

I was the last in line with our small group as we made our way to the order station. Just before my turn came, I looked around and noticed an elderly couple headed my way. They had said nothing to me, and I'm not even sure they took notice of me, but without warning, I felt like letting loose with a string of obscenities at them. Fortunately, I kept silent, and whatever was being stirred up in me gradually settled down. I was a prison inmate and for a moment felt if they knew, they would be afraid.

I could be wrong, but when I found myself in the presence of non-prison people (outsiders), I saw my identity as an inmate, a resident of the state's prison system – an outcast to be feared. I was not one of them, an outsider. I was the product of what I had done to put me in prison. I was a sex offender!

After my release, I thought I would see prison life as history, something that I could put behind me as I continued my journey. That's not the way things went, however. I don't think I ever said anything out loud, but every now and then I heard a voice inside me yelling, "Unclean, unclean!" like some leper banished to isolation.

Self-Identity

Change and Anxiety

I don't advertise the fact that I spent time in prison, although if I am asked, I say yes. After all, my situation is a matter of public record. There are also several internet search programs for those wanting to know if any sex offenders live nearby. I entered my address in one of them and was surprised by how many registrants lived within a few blocks of me.

There are people all around, obviously. Some of us are on the registry, but most are not, so worrying about being "found out" is a waste of energy. Not long ago, someone said to me, "I know about your past." And she did. The key word she used was "past," a word that should not negatively affect me unless my current choices mirror those from that past.

2

Getting Closer

Program Review Committee
The PRC

In Wisconsin, meeting with this committee of staff members was usually a formality, a time to evaluate a job assignment or any behavior issues that might have resulted in receiving a disciplinary ticket.

In the 80s, Wisconsin prisons operated on a mandatory-release formula (inmates served two-thirds of their sentence). I was nearing that point in my own sentence, and the panel wanted to discuss what I hoped to do once I was released from prison. My charges ruled out any chance of teaching, but I also knew I had no experience in construction, plumbing, or any other similar occupation. I was, however, interested in computer-related options.

After answering questions for about 30 minutes, I was sent out of the room to await their decision. When called back in, I was told that they were recommending a transfer to a Milwaukee halfway house where I would be allowed to attend classes at nearby Milwaukee Area Technical College (MATC).

SAYING GOODBYE

I don't remember where the advice came from, but someone had told me, "Don't just leave. Don't just turn your back on everyone and everything here. Say goodbye. Tell people that they have made a difference in your life. You need to do that."

He was right. More than one person inside helped me through

a difficult time, allowed me to share what I was feeling, listened as I spoke of God's leading, or encouraged me to believe things would be okay. Just as I suppose I had done for them without knowing I had. Those people deserved to know they mattered, and they did.

The same truth applied to some of the staff members, both security and administrative. In prison, it is easy to develop a 'we-they' attitude. I knew some staff members who certainly were not good people, but I also knew some who were great people. Serving as a Business Office clerk, one of my supervisors told me, "If you ever come back to this place, I am going to see you never leave that desk you worked at for me." He trusted me, gave me responsibilities beyond the normal assigned tasks, and challenged me.

One evening, security stopped by my room and said, "Pack up. You leave tomorrow." This time, my belongings filled several boxes, and I wondered how I had gotten so rich in possessions.

When the transport van bringing another inmate and me arrived at the Milwaukee halfway house, I realized that most of my property didn't make the journey. They assured me, though, that it would be delivered within a week. I certainly hoped it would because the only underclothing I had was what I was wearing at the time.

Fortunately, the halfway house was within 20 miles of my home. I was given permission to call my wife and, thank God, she was allowed to bring me what I needed.

School: A God Story

Sometimes I tell someone, "I'll pray for you" or "God will meet your needs," and the other person is probably thinking, "Yeah, right." What God does is what God does, but I believe I have never been left unaided. My prayers are not a formula guaranteed to have God snap his fingers and make my prayer request a reality. But this story really happened, and I want to share it with you.

At my new home, I had just finished making the bed I had been assigned when the desk sergeant called me into his office.

"Tomorrow morning, the van taking guys from here to the pallet company will leave at 7:00. You will be on it."

"But PRC recommended me to attend MATC for computer courses."

"That's not going to happen," he responded.

"I would appreciate you checking with the warden and looking at the paperwork that I gave you."

He didn't smile, and I didn't expect him to. I was also surprised at how bold I had sounded.

An hour later, the desk sergeant called me back in.

"Here's the deal," he said. "Tomorrow, you will leave here at 9:00 AM, walk to MATC using the route you will be given, and be back here by noon. If you are unable to register, you will either join the pallet crew, or I will have you returned to Oakhill Correctional. Is that understood? And don't even think about going a different route from the one I have given you!"

"Yes" was all I could answer.

The next morning, I managed to find the school using the route I was told to follow, but I was almost certain that I was being followed. Just my imagination, I decided. As I stepped inside the main lobby, I was overwhelmed by all the people who, I quickly learned, were registering for classes that would start *the following day*.

All I felt in that moment was that I was unable to do anything. I stood frozen in place and even started crying.

An older man I had not previously noticed came out of an office and asked, "Is there anything I can do for you?"

Without considering what I was saying, I answered, "I just got transferred from Oakhill Correctional to the halfway house here, and I only have a few more hours to get registered, or I go back."

"What courses do you want to take?"

"I was thinking about computer, but I'm not sure."

He walked me into a room where schedule sheets were taped to every available space. He looked from one sheet to another and then at me. "You're out of luck as far as computers are concerned. All the intro classes are full. Is there anything else that might interest you?"

"Well," I said, "I have always been good with numbers."

He turned back to the walls and then started copying down information.

"You're in luck. All the classes you need for accounting are available."

He then handed me the slip of paper and pointed me toward a

line of students who had formed, waiting to register. I handed the slip of paper over when my turn finally came up.

She said, "This is fine. How will you be paying for this?"

It was at that moment that I realized I had no ID and no wallet, much less any money to put in a wallet if I had one.

The only thing I could think of saying was what I had shared with the other man.

She said, "Just a moment," picked up the phone, and asked me to stand off to the side and wait for someone who might be able to help me.

Minutes later, I was sitting in an office facing a woman who asked me to share my circumstances. Once more, I offered my current situation. Her response caught me off guard.

"I know who you are. My children attended the high school where you taught. I know all about your arrest."

There was a pause before she looked at me and said, "Let's see what we can do."

A call home confirmed that the fees would be covered. But this kind woman also gave me a voucher to cover the costs of the books I would need the next day.

To myself, I was saying, "Praise God, thank you, God!" over and over.

When I walked into the desk sergeant's office at 11:45, he looked up and reminded me of the schedule at the pallet company.

I lifted the bag of books and said, "But I have three classes tomorrow." I don't think he was happy, but I was.

God's responses to our prayers are the gifts of love he shares with all of us, each as our needs require.

Parole Granted

My first semester at school was going well. A plus came in the form of visits from my wife and family. It was no longer an hour-plus drive to come and see me – a blessing that reminds me that this woman was more than I deserved.

One day, a three-member parole panel came to the halfway house, and I was scheduled for some of their time. A friend had reminded me that I needed to answer the questions asked in a parole hearing as truthfully as possible. I had thought that I would need to have all the right answers to prove that I was worth a parole, but I let go of that idea when I realized I wasn't expected to have all the answers. I was just expected to answer.

The board asked what I had learned while in prison and in treatment. They also asked whether I felt I was ready to start over.

At one point, the questions just stopped. Then I heard, "We're going to give you a parole." There was a pause before they continued. "We are also confident that you will respect our decision by continuing what you need to do in your commitment to making change in your life."

Feeling somewhat stunned, I said, "Thank you!"

Out in the hall, I saw my best friend waiting for me, and he held me as I cried. I know; "Real men don't cry" is what people say, but in a situation like this, the experience is a bit overwhelming and, I think, tears are an appropriate response.

Remembering to say "Thank you."

In the few weeks before leaving the halfway house, I remembered to thank those who were important to me during this time. I was also able to share the joy I felt with some of my teachers at MATC. And yes, I was able to thank those who made MATC possible for me. God's gifts – all of them.

Sadly, there are individuals who are granted parole, expecting they will be back in prison. For them, there is no joy felt in hearing "Parole granted." But for every person I've met who really wanted a chance to start over, the joy that follows a board's positive decision is awesome!

"Don't Be Afraid, Just Believe!" (ITL)

[35]While Jesus was still speaking, some men came from the house of Jairus, the synagogue ruler. "Your daughter is dead," they said. "Why bother the teacher anymore?"

[36]Ignoring what they said, Jesus told the synagogue ruler, "Don't be afraid; just believe."

[37]He did not let anyone follow him except Peter, James, and John, the brother of James. [38]When they came to the home of the synagogue ruler, Jesus saw a commotion, with people crying and wailing loudly. [39]He went in and said to them, "Why all this commotion and wailing? The child is not dead but asleep." [40]But they laughed at him.

After he put them all out, he took the child's father and mother and the disciples who were with him and went in where the child was. [41]He took her by the hand and said to her, "Talitha koum!" which means, "Little girl, I say to you, get up!." [42]Immediately the girl stood up and walked around (she was twelve years old). At this they were completely astonished.

Mark 5:35-42 NIV

Sometimes we read or listen to the Gospel with too much familiarity because the text has a "been there, heard that" feel to it. Yet Jesus said, "*18Having eyes, do you not see? And having ears, do you not hear? And do you not remember?*" (Mark 8:18). When we gloss over the Word or listen with a wandering mind, we have neither eyes nor ears.

As I washed up early that morning while listening to the news, I listened to three reports being aired involving child molestation cases. I immediately thought, "How does any registrant stand a chance of getting help once out of prison? The odds seem to be completely against anyone with sex-related charges because of all that is happening, all the anger that is building."

Looking at the gospel verses for that day, I knew I was going to be in something of a "been there, know that" frame of mind. I skimmed rather than really read the story of Jairus and his dying daughter from start to finish. Somehow, the words "*Don't be afraid; just believe*" caught my attention and called me back for a second look.

They were simple words, yet powerful words. "*Don't be afraid; just believe.*" Jesus heard what the men were saying to Jairus about his daughter. He knew the despair Jairus must have been feeling. After all, this was a father who loved his daughter so much that he sought out Jesus to come and heal her. At that moment, Jesus didn't focus on the men bearing their message. He merely told Jairus not to be afraid. He told him to believe.

Jon (just a name I've chosen) wrote to me the other week. He was nearing the end of his sentence and was currently completing a sex offender treatment program. Jon wasn't sure where he would be living, who would hire him, or where he would be able to attend worship services. Near the end of his letter, Jon shared how each day he prayed to God, asking for help and healing. He knew that he had changed in many ways, yet "out there" was the unknown, a place that was more than a little frightening for Jon.

In a way, Jon represents both Jairus and his daughter. As Jairus, he daily approaches the altar of God with his plea for healing. In the thinking of most who knew him, Jon's prayers for healing were considered a waste of time. They loudly proclaimed, "Once a child molester, always a child molester. Why bother God with your prayers?"

Yet Jon had faith—the kind of faith that prompted Jairus to

search Jesus out. And in response to Jon's prayers, I believe that Jesus said the same thing to Jon that He did to Jairus: "*Don't be afraid; just believe.*" Jon believes, but he is still afraid. Why? Perhaps some other elements of the story of Jairus and his daughter might provide some thoughts to consider.

"Your daughter is dead," they said.

From the first day until the last day of Jon's time in prison, he felt completely separated from those on the outside. His wife divorced him, his brothers and sisters refused any communication with him, and his pastor had "cast him out" of the congregation. Completely cut off from the outside world, Jon felt as though he were dead.

Jesus saw a commotion, with people crying and wailing loudly.

As Jon imagined what it would be like to leave prison and start life over, he envisioned the news broadcasts he had seen where townspeople protested at a city council meeting. They were protesting a registrant moving into one of their neighborhoods, and he saw himself as that man.

The concerns people expressed to the elected officials were not shared in calm voices. Their words surfaced as angry shouts punctuated by raised fists. Jon did not know that what he saw on TV was the exception rather than the rule - only a very small percentage of released offenders find themselves the object of such a meeting. But because Jon didn't know this, the fear he had was very real.

The child is not dead but asleep …

In Jon's quiet moments, his prayer time, and in his communion with God, he saw a glimmer of hope and the possibility of reentering the world as a new man. In those quiet moments, he understood that his homecoming would not be a parade down Main Street. It would be an obstacle course.

How everything would fall into place once on the streets was beyond his vision because that vision was one of housing, job opportunities, and church membership. But the bottom line was that the vision he came to rely on was really a vision built on faith and trust. It was the belief that God had a purpose for his life.

But they laughed at him...

Bible scholars say that when the friends of Jairus heard Jesus say the girl was merely sleeping, they laughed, but it was scornful laughter. They had seen the dead girl. Jesus had not. How could He say she was only asleep?

The accounts in the newspapers had declared Jon a child molester and pedophile. The conviction and the sentencing had confirmed this identity as Jon's, and in the mind of the public, there was nothing more to add. It was an identity that could not be changed. "Bleeding heart liberals" would say that it might be possible for a registrant to be rehabilitated, but what did they know? For every such person who stood on Jon's side, hundreds stood opposed and were more than willing to scorn him.

Little girl, I say to you, get up!

This is the bottom line for Jon. This is the command from God that he hears in his heart, a command that flies in the face of all the opposition that might and will come against him. It is a command that says, "I know your struggle, Jon, but I do know that your identity is fixed in me, not in your offenses. Get up!"

It is also a command that acknowledges the condition that still exists within Jon, a condition that he must monitor daily to avoid hurting another child. God's command is one of healing and not condemnation, encouragement and not ridicule.

The journey Jon is making is far from easy, but God has already arranged for him to meet help along the way. He has promised Jon that He will always be with him, helping him deal with the difficult times and showing him how to rejoice in the good times. And in the end, Jon will have stood up, a man clothed in both the love and presence of the Lord. Those who look on Jon will be astonished because the man they considered dead had come to life!

Tucked inside the story of Jairus and Jon are two important words: get up! Nothing changes if we don't act. Nothing changes if we hide in a corner, hoping no one notices us. And nothing changes if we say "I believe, Lord," yet allow fear to dictate our lives.

Some people I once called friends might never be so again. I can't force them to be my friends. My participation at church still has restrictions. The restrictions make others feel more comfortable and, I suppose, feel more protected, though that confuses me and saddens me. How they respond to me, however, is a direct consequence of the choices I made that hurt so many.

I am still a little afraid, but I am not paralyzed by my fears. I believe with all my being because God has done so much for me: *He lifted me out of the slimy pit, out of the mud and mire; he set my feet on a rock and gave me a firm place to stand.* (Psalm 40:2 NIV)

You might not 'feel' the same at this very moment. But if you ask God to show you, He will open your eyes to all the many miracles He has already worked in your life, and He'll remind you that He is not done with you!

Part Two
First Days Out

Things that are New Ways

What Standing Count?

One of the things I often hear from those in reentry is the joy of knowing there is no more standing count. No more waiting to be counted as present whenever security decided to call for a count. One man wrote that on his first morning out, he stood outside his bedroom door waiting for his name to be called. Of course, that was the only time it happened, but it happened.

Jeans, Panic, and Institutional Thinking

Needing some jeans, my son and I went to our local Goodwill store to pick out a pair. After walking around a bit, he pointed to tables piled up high with jeans of all sizes. Nothing was neatly arranged by size or sorted on hangers, and as I stared at the tables, I panicked. My son came up alongside, took me by the arm, and said, "Dad, let's get out of here."

Once home, I tried to tell my wife what had happened, but the moment I revisited the image of that mess, I was mentally back in front of those piles. Then I started to lose it again.

When I finally settled down, I made a guess of what had happened. Instead of order, I had seen chaos. Instead of clear options, in my mind, I had none. Then it hit me. Inside prison, my clothes were handed to me. No questions. No choices. It was drab green or drab green – oh, and for variation, washed-out brown. I did fight, however, for socks whose elastics still had enough life to hold them up.

Meals in prison were whatever someone said they'd be. We got up and went to bed when told. In short, though we were able to choose some things, most of the time, others made decisions for us.

I had never really understood what institutional thinking was until I experienced it. Fortunately, whenever I feel that panic rising, I have a good idea of what was behind it, and I cope much better.

My Friend Fredricks

While I was on parole, three weeks were remaining in my first semester at Milwaukee Area Technical College.

Our home was about 20 miles from the school, my wife was working, and I had no car. For those final three weeks, I walked to a bus stop a few blocks from my home, took a bus to the downtown terminal, and then boarded a transfer bus that took me within a block of the campus in Milwaukee. After school, it was just the reverse.

Attending classes was not a problem because the only people I interacted with were teachers, other students in my classes, and cafeteria staff. Only a few really knew my circumstances, and that limited knowledge worked for me.

A few days before the start of the next semester, my wife and I went to enroll at nearby Waukesha County Technical College. We had just entered the building when a voice called, "Hey, Van Domelen!" Then this man started quickly moving toward us. Once he was out of the shadows, we both recognized that it was Tom Fredricks, an old family friend.

As things happened, he taught upper-level accounting and tax courses at the college, and I would eventually have him as an instructor. This reconnection was a pleasant thought, but it paled in comparison to his honest expression of joy at seeing me. His hug was not forced, and in that moment, I think some of the tension inside me disappeared a little.

Tom then took me to one of the registration windows and loudly told the clerk, "Take care of my friend here!" Looking at the clerk, I realized she had been a student of mine some years back. I remembered the instrument she played, where she sat in her section, and the many times I disrupted conversations she was having with the girl sitting next to her. I didn't say it out loud, but I thought to myself, "All this is another God thing." There was no reason to believe it wasn't.

The point I am making is that it is one thing to move among strangers and another to be with people who are not. I think in most of the encounters with people I knew, I felt a sense of shame. Sometimes I physically turned away to avoid the awkwardness, and sometimes I saw people doing the same. Yet if there was any awkwardness on Tom's part, he didn't show it. When he passed away a few years ago, I knew I had lost a good friend.

Reentry might have been much easier, I think, if my crime had not been what it was. I can't speak for people charged with different felonies, but as a registrant, the barriers and uneasiness others had in my presence are real. And unavoidable.

6

Thoughts from Registrants

I asked readers of *Into the Light*,
"Describe your first days out (good things, problems, etc.)

Hectic. I had to register, see probation, obtain a driver's license, and make an appointment with Social Security. Obtained a phone and applied for the food assistance program. My close associate drove me around and assisted in the matters at hand, as he had the same experiences when he was released from prison three years ago.

***

As I walked out the gate, it was with a mix of emotions. In the seven years I was there, I became part of a wonderful Christian family, and I felt a little sad leaving them. As a matter of fact, I felt odd being outside the prison.

My first day out was a bit scary, wondering how the halfway house ran, if there would be your usual haters and typical hierarchy, and if staff would allow that. But being able to put together breakfast in the kitchen (toasting waffles and getting a cup of real coffee) felt great. Freedom had not really settled in, but I felt a weight removed.

I was, however, a bit concerned because I would have to start a new life. There were one or two people I knew from prison there, and they helped me. The staff was good, no politics or issues, and after my first day, I was able to get an hour's pass to shop for supplies. My family lived over an hour away, and they gave me a whole bunch of clothes and stuff, but I still needed some things we forgot.

***

The first time I got out, I walked to the gas station where I bought myself a pack of cigs and a Coca-Cola. My social worker told me before I left the institution that I could not afford to smoke cigs, but I did not listen. When I got out the second time, it was February, and I soon noticed that a lot of the smokers were coughing. I didn't know if the coughing was because of the cold or the cigs.

***

Two friends I had not seen in years offered to pick me up. They were a few hours late, but I kept cool reading until I was finally called up. They brought me some really nice clothes and some nice jackets, too. I am very blessed. I felt like I was in a dream. It was hard to believe I was really out, and maybe in some ways I am still in shock.

We stopped at a Roy Rogers restaurant on the turnpike. I had a roast beef sandwich for my first meal. It was a strange feeling being in there. I was afraid to go to the bathroom by myself at first. I guess I thought I had to be "supervised."

When we made it to the Center where I would be staying, I was really shocked. No sooner did I introduce myself, give my papers, and sign in than the Monitor (officer) told me I could sign out for two hours. Wow! I didn't know I would have freedom like that, especially so soon.

That evening, two others and I, who had arrived that day, had an orientation meeting where the rules were explained to us. I could go out for two hours at a time and was allowed to have a bicycle or a car. The staff here seems fair and respectable, too. My first night, I couldn't fall asleep because I was so excited. When I finally did, I didn't wake up until 8:00 a.m.—the latest I have slept in years.

After taking the right bus in the wrong direction, I finally made it to the parole office and saw my agent. The interview went well. I was kind of surprised when I asked about what job restrictions there might be—he said, "Just use common sense." I asked him about the inadvertent contact issue. He said that if I happen to encounter a child who talks to me or touches me, I should report it.

I came home from group, and one of the guys told me that the staff had searched my property. I didn't think anything of it because I knew I didn't have contraband. There was a confiscation slip, however, that showed that they had taken my photo albums, drawings, a catalog, a tape series titled "Love Won Out," as well as several books and booklets—including "Help for Adults Attracted to Children." Needless to say, I did not get much sleep that night, worrying over what this was all about.

At a meeting the next day, I walked in to see the director of the center and my counselor, my therapist, and my parole agent were all present. I knew that this was very serious. The things taken were thrown on the table, and the therapist asked what I was doing with pictures of children. He stated I was not to have any pictures of children whatsoever. Because the pictures were of family relatives, I didn't even consider them to be inappropriate or falling under any prohibitive rules.

I had to relinquish the tracts and ministry magazines that had any pictures of children in them, and I will not be able to receive any such magazines in the future. The drawings I had made of some of the pictures angered the therapist, as one of the drawings was of a victim.

My therapist wanted to "discharge" me at that point, and that would have meant I was in violation of parole, but he decided to give me a chance since everything on the table had come with me from prison. This will mean, however, that I will be under special scrutiny, especially my mail.

***

I was very excited. Joy at seeing friends and talking to people without having the prison recording in the background. I felt a little anxious about starting over. Will I be accepted?

***

My first day out was the most challenging. I was nervous as I had not been told my parole site had been approved, just "Go pack your things. You're leaving tomorrow." But it was actually today.

My friend came to pick me up – great to see him after so many years. Not knowing what his home was like, however, was nerve-racking. Calling into the Illinois Department of Corrections to inform them I was released and at home was hard, as I had to follow prompts using a cell phone. Never owned one.

***

In my first days out, I had a lot of trouble sleeping and eating normally. I was physically sick a couple of times from anxiety, even though I know the friend I live with. Using my own personal phone, showering when I wanted, making my own schedule, etc, all take time to get used to.

***

When I first got set free from a civil commitment program, I was in shock. This was an entirely different world from the one I left 17 years ago.

"Remember Me" (ITL)

Remember not the sins of my youth or my transgressions;
according to your steadfast love remember me,
for the sake of your goodness, O Lord!

Psalm 25:7 ESV

A little more than a year ago, I received a letter from a man who was nearing the end of his court-ordered sentence. He shared briefly about his concerns about getting a job or finding a place to live, but added that those would eventually happen.

What concerned him most was returning to his hometown, walking down the street, and seeing people go out of their way to avoid contact with him. He imagined them saying, "There's that pervert. What's he doing here?"

For them, he would no longer be recognized as the man who used to work at the hardware store or the neighbor always willing to lend a hand when something needed doing. For them, the good things he had done before his arrest were forgotten, and all that he might have done in prison to change wouldn't make a difference because they didn't care.

He closed his letter by adding, "What difference does it make if I am an outcast? I might as well molest a child again and get sent back to prison. It's what everyone expects of me. Why should I disappoint them?" I answered his letter, but I don't know if it did any good.

I haven't heard from him since that letter. Still, I think of him often and pray that he is doing well. Most of all, I pray that he is being encouraged by people who really care about him, people who remember him working at the hardware store, people who remember the many times he helped others out.

His letter was one of identity – how he saw himself and how he believed society would see him once he was released. This is a question I have thought about quite often over the years, and I am convinced that how I see myself is the most important choice.

Remember not the sins of my youth or my transgressions…

Without hesitation, I can drag up my past sins. I can see the harm that I have brought to the lives of so many, the trust I destroyed in pursuit of my own choices. There was a time I believed I would never be able to move beyond those memories, and if I couldn't, then I was destined to be lost in my own 'mud and mire.' (Psalm 40)

David's prayer was my prayer, for I knew that God was the only one who could put things right. Yes, I had to accept the consequences of my actions, acknowledging that I had no control over what that might look like, but I pleaded that what I had done would not define my identity in God's eyes.

The change from my distorted image of myself to one that spoke of God's presence in my life didn't happen overnight. At some point during my time in prison, a chaplain shared a verse that remains one of my favorites.

"For I know the plans I have for you," declares the Lord,
"plans to prosper you and not to harm you, plans to give you
hope and a future."

(Jeremiah 29:11 NIV)

If God had plans for me, I had to believe they would be better than any I might envision for myself. And they are!

… according to your steadfast love
remember me…

Sometimes, I think we all expect God to act as we think he *should*, but we base those expectations on experiences we have had with others in our lives. If we push a best friend too hard, eventually we will be minus a best friend. It's how we humans respond to one another.

But God says, *"Never will I leave you; never will I forsake you"* (Hebrews 13:5 NIV). That sounds to me like a very serious commitment, one that I decided I could believe, one that gives my journey meaning and purpose.

Some translations use "according to your steadfast mercy." I don't believe that one can love without mercy; one cannot have mercy, real and complete, without love; and Jesus is the only one who lived among us who is capable of both. That brings me to how we see ourselves and how God sees us.

The man who wrote me feared his release because of how he believed others identified him – a pervert. This fear grew to the point where he felt he had no choice but to reoffend. It was what he believed others expected of him. I can understand how he came to believe that distortion. I just can't identify with it.

Here's a simple reality for you to consider. If a man with a past that included molestation entered a room filled with ministers, there would still be at least one minister who had strong reservations about this man being allowed in that group setting. This minister might speak words of welcome, but those words would be at odds with how he really felt.

Our job is not to convince the world that we have changed – someone will always deny that such a change has occurred. We are, however, called to open our lives to God's mercy and love. When our choices are based on the examples Jesus provided, our lives will reflect change, not because we *tell* people we have changed, but because we *have* changed.

> After removing Saul, he made David their king. God testified concerning him: 'I have found David son of Jesse, a man after my own heart; he will do everything I want him to do.'

> Acts 13:22 NIV

This is how God sees us. This is an example of the love and mercy shown to David, a love and mercy that changed David's identity from adulterer and murderer to *"a man after my own heart."*

… for the sake of your goodness, O Lord!

Why would God extend love and mercy? Why would God overlook David's sins/crimes? Our sins/crimes? He does all of this because it is in his nature to do so. He wants you and me to spend eternity with him in paradise.

[39] One of the criminals who hung there hurled insults at him: "Aren't you the Messiah? Save yourself and us!" [40] But the other criminal rebuked him. "Don't you fear God," he said, "since you are under the same sentence? [41] We are punished justly, for we are getting what our deeds deserve. But this man has done nothing wrong." [42] Then he said, "Jesus, *remember me* when you come into your kingdom." [43] Jesus answered him, *"Truly I tell you, today you will be with me in paradise."*

Luke 23:39-43 NIV

Jesus did not say, "I don't think I can do that because there are a lot of people who want me to send you to hell." He said what he did because the man recognized and admitted his failings. Most of all because the man asked. And so, I say, "Jesus, remember me!"

Part Three

Meeting Basic Needs: A Home

7

Home - a Place to Live

I was paroled in late 1988 and was incredibly blessed to be able to return to my family home. Some years later, Wisconsin signed into law the Wisconsin Sex Offender Registry Program (SORP), a law whose purpose was to track those with sex related offenses living in the state.

In 2006, the Adam Walsh Child Protection and Safety Act was enacted nationally, and the following year, communities across the country began creating residency restriction laws for registrants. These community laws banned registrants from living within a set distance of a restricted area—schools, parks, childcare centers— places where children were apt to congregate. The distance can vary; it should be noted that distance is always a straight line.

When I first became involved in jail and prison ministry, finding a place to live was not the problem it is today. Families might have taken the welcome mat away, landlords probably rejected any ex-felon, but with residency restriction laws came a legal way to refuse a registrant the right to live anywhere inside most city limits.

Few weeks go by without a letter or sometimes a call asking me for help finding a place to live. Most of the time, it is a letter from a registrant nearing a release date, but on occasion, the inquirer is a family member or a friend.

Phone conversations usually begin, "I heard that you might be able to help. Our son is getting out of prison soon. Do you know of apartments or places willing to rent to an ex-felon?"

I have learned that my first question needs to be, "Will he be on the state registry?" The answer tells me if his charges are sex-related or not, and if they are, what I share is the information I have specific to their son's needs. Often, the best I can do is offer them information they might have already tried without success.

INTERNET RESOURCES

If you are reading this and have internet access, the following links offer practical suggestions for finding housing, as well as embedded links with information on other needs.

https://Helpforfelons.org
Practical advice for not only housing but also employment and financial suggestions.
How to Find Housing as a Registered Person – Once Fallen
https://oncefallen.com/finding-housing/
Good information on many topics, but the site has a small print default that you might want to adjust.
Housing For Sex Offenders Near Me 2025 Updated
https://rentingtofelons.org/housing/sexoffenders/
Helpful steps and suggestions offered.

Before state registries or local residency restriction laws, halfway houses or transitional living arrangements created by Departments of Corrections were common. Initially, they placed these facilities in locations where public transportation was available, enabling registrants a way to get to work.

However, in most communities, those locations were found to be in violation of residency restrictions laws, given their proximity to schools, churches, childcare centers, and parks or playgrounds. As a result, many correctional institutions began to approach release differently.

Many now require that a registrant present a pre-release plan for approval before release is granted. While the content of these plans can vary, the following information must be included:

- Address - specifics required as the address must be approved by a local agent.
- Employment – company, address, and work assignment.
- Support system in place – group, family, friends.

- Treatment – state-run program for registrants in reentry.

This request might be very doable for some but impossible for others. The process becomes more complicated if someone is still in confinement with limited access to the outside world. To see this somewhat differently, let me offer an example, one free of correctional institution requirements.

THE IMPORTANCE OF AN ADDRESS

Graduating from college and entering the business world in a new location comes with more than a few complications for non-incarcerated young adults.

Before a college diploma is even in hand, most individuals are likely to have completed a successful job search, found an apartment in the new job location, and, God willing, made a connection with a new church family.

Financially, that new apartment will need to be secured with a security deposit check. Usually, an existing bank account works, but opening a new bank account is a better, long-term choice.

These are steps most young adults face when starting their new lives following college. Imagine these same steps if you are in prison and are not allowed internet use, much less the ability to physically go from company to company for those still doing face-to-face interviews, or going from apartment to apartment seeking a fit for your needs.

The biggest issue, however, remains finding a place to live. In some cases, that might mean staying with family members or friends with the parole agent's approval. The internet sites listed earlier offer the kind of suggestions and steps that may make finding a place easier, but they will not make the process easy.

If you are applying for a job, an address will likely be required on the application form. Homeless shelters sometimes allow an individual to temporarily use their address until a personal address is found. If possible, consider gathering this information *before* you start your job search.

I asked readers of *Into the Light*,
"Describe finding a place to live."

The township where I had hoped to live told me I could not live there, but I could within the county. My wife and I then began the search for a residence where I could live. We did find a house we could purchase and, with a little tender loving care, we made this house into a home for the two of us. I had been semi-retired before prison, so when I was released, things were bearable.

***

Unable to find a place to live, I talked to my sister and my brother about renting their cottage, which was a better place to live during the winter months. When spring came, my cousin helped me find a place at a trailer park. I have been living there for seven years now and am happy to say I own this two-bedroom trailer house.

***

It was extremely frustrating and nerve-racking to the point of my being ready to throw in the towel and completely give up. I wrote over 20 letters to different places, receiving very few responses. My close associate was called by my attorney, who had finally located a place to reside. I was released by the courts in July of 2024, but my getting a residence did not happen until February 2025.

***

Luckily, I had eight months in a halfway house to adjust. I thank God my sister has a large house with a finished lower level that I can have, even though I make her take my rent. I have privacy when I want, and we share the kitchen.

***

I transitioned from a halfway house to renting without any difficulties.

***

I was fortunate to have a friend who I met while incarcerated, who was willing and able to allow me to parole and stay with. Finding places that meet SO requirements is not easy, but it's not impossible.

***

As a child, I saw how others experienced homelessness in our small town. We lived near railroad tracks, and there would be campsites where hobos would gather and cook food and drink alcohol. My mother used to make biscuits and always made a big one that she called a hobo biscuit to offer anyone who came to our door looking for food.

Because of a previous offense, I was grandfathered into our family home, which was a blessing. This state does not have many places you can go if you don't have a relative or someone willing to take you in. Wherever you stay has to be approved by the Sex Offender Registry Office.

***

I pray I find permanent housing before my two years are up. The "Stand Down" offered free clothes, food, counseling, help finding housing, everything from soap to razors, shampoo, and all the things you would make yourself look good with. I even got a free haircut. When I got back to where I am staying and unpacked all my gifts, it felt like Christmas in October.

"Come to Me" (ITL)

28 "Come to me, all you who are weary and burdened, and I will give you rest. 29 Take my yoke upon you and learn from me, for I am gentle and humble in heart, and you will find rest for your souls. 30 For my yoke is easy and my burden is light."

Matthew 11:28-30

Several years ago, I was invited to offer a workshop at what was then called the Central Illinois Sunday School and Church Mission Conference in Peoria, IL.

Having arrived early, I decided to take a little walk to deal with the anxiety I was beginning to feel. I didn't get too far, though. Across the street from the Peoria Civic Center was a church; that's where I headed.

After sitting quietly in one of the back pews, I left by a side door and found myself facing a life-sized statue of Jesus. I felt a wave of peace flow over me. Inscribed on a plaque at the base of the statue was Matthew 11:28-30. I knew things would be fine, as those words are among the core verses for my ministry.

[28] "Come to me, all you who are weary and burdened, and I will give you rest. [29] Take my yoke upon you and learn from me, for I am gentle and humble in heart, and you will find rest for your souls. [30] For my yoke is easy and my burden is light."

Back at the Civic Center, I located the room I was assigned to and verified my workshop time, then headed to see the exhibits.

While walking around, I heard an announcement that there were changes to the schedule, so I approached the information tables to learn what they were.

It was a surprise to learn that not only had my workshop time been changed from 3:00 PM to 7:00 PM, but that there was a room change as well. *That* change took me by surprise because my workshop was not even in the Civic Center. I was now scheduled to speak on the fourth floor of the City Hall Building next to the Center. On entering that building, I could see that the only way to the assigned room was either taking a small elevator or by climbing the stairs.

Panic began to take hold. How could anyone find this room? How would such a small elevator meet the needs of the number I hoped would be attending? Yet in some spot deep within, I remembered the plaque—Matthew 11:28-30—and decided to trust God.

Despite the change of time and location, the workshop was a success, and the City Council Chamber was filled that evening. I did remember to share all of this with those who attended – because we are called to share how God blesses us.

Come to me, all you who are weary and burdened ...

I was a teenager the first time I felt drawn to these words because I *was* weary and I certainly *was* burdened. Maybe at the time I believed that the attractions I struggled with would disappear; maybe they were just a phase I was going through. But the more I prayed, the more aware I became of the grip those issues had on me.

My memories are filled with hours spent in church, singing in the choir, and listening to God's word preached – sometimes with passion, sometimes not, but God's word all the same. And on those occasions, I did feel that my darkness was less controlling, and my spirit had found a measure of peace. But it wasn't a lasting peace.

... and I will give you rest.

I wanted those words to be real. I wanted that rest. But I wanted that rest to be freedom from the growing panic my behaviors brought on. "I believe, Lord! Just say the words! *Say the words!*" I didn't hear them - but eventually I would.

I know that I am not alone – many of you have written of the times you called to God for deliverance, only to feel that God wasn't listening. But our faith tells us He was. In the Garden of Gethsemane, Jesus prayed, "Yet not as I will but as you will" (Matthew 26:39). Should our prayer be any less? Should our surrender be any less complete?

> *Take my yoke upon you and learn from me*
> *for I am gentle and humble in heart,*
> *and you will find rest for your souls.*

verse 29

Jesus called the laws placed on the Jewish people by the Pharisees a yoke laid on the shoulders of others by those unwilling to help carry them. The yoke Jesus asks us to take on is the yoke of turning from our sinful choices and of asking for the faith that includes a heartfelt desire to follow Him. There are no guarantees of a tension-free life, no promises that we will not have struggles. Jesus knows this and still offers us an invitation to follow him – *take my yoke.*

Take and *learn* are action verbs, words that demand a mental response as well as a sense of active participation. Someone can hold out a gift to us, and we can appreciate the gesture, but unless we reach out and take it, that gift is not ours.

Jesus is saying to each of us, "I know what you have done, the harm you have caused, and the lives that have been changed by your actions, but I still love you. Let me touch those parts of you that need healing. Let me show you how to be sorry. I can bring you back to life in me. Just tell me that you are willing to let me walk with you!"

All change is a process, and lasting behavior change and thinking can be a lengthy process. I think we have all felt moments of freedom from those yokes of destruction we carry. And I am pretty sure that when temptation of *any* kind begins to torment us, we wonder where the sense of freedom went. "Maybe," we tell ourselves, "change isn't possible. Maybe this is how I will always be." But the words in Matthew 11:28-30 are not merely a suggestion. They are a promise. We *will* find rest. Because Jesus said we would.

For my yoke is easy and my burden is light.

For many, the decision to surrender to God and to acknowledge Jesus as our Lord and Savior is seen as the beginning of a long, hard journey. Maybe that's because we all tend to focus too much on the "Thou shalt not" parts instead of looking at what this relationship will mean to our well-being and happiness.

When we walk in the law of the Lord, we become more aware of the presence of the Holy Spirit, and our focus increasingly leans toward the positive rather than the negative.

In Paul's letter to the Galatians (5:22-23), he points out what we have to look forward to: *22 But the fruit of the Spirit is love, joy, peace, forbearance, kindness, goodness, faithfulness, 23 gentleness and self-control.* While we can all appreciate the first eight, I think the gift of self-control we understand and desire but often seems just out of reach.

Treatment programs focus on what we have done and what steps we need to take to avoid making the same choices. That is certainly an important goal, one that society hopes we have achieved before reentry. But a weakness in such programs is that focusing on the past alone will not lead to change until we have a positive image of the new person we hope to be. We must see ourselves as God sees us.

That will take time and commitment, but it will also require that we trust God to be with us. As I have shared repeatedly over the years, if we define ourselves by the nature of our sins, we will always live from the center of that sin identity. If, however, we are willing to take His yoke and to learn from him, we *will* find rest. We will also find the identity in God that we were always meant to have.

Come to me, all you who are weary and burdened. Is that you? Is that me? Some days, I am pretty sure we all feel that way. The invitation is there. How about it?

Part Four

Meeting Basic Needs: Work

8

A Place to Work

It would be great to say companies are just waiting for the next registrant to apply, but that isn't true. Anyone who suggests anything like that knows less than you or me. That isn't to say there aren't available jobs, and yes, being a registrant makes them harder to find, but registrants ultimately jump through the same hoops as everyone else.

In theory, being a registrant doesn't automatically close the door on all types of employment, but those doors will be closed if your offense is in any way related to your desired employment. The following additional information is taken from a search on the internet listing some professions with their doors <u>closed</u> to registrants:

> <u>Government Jobs</u>: Positions within federal law enforcement and the U.S. military are off-limits to all felons due to federal statutes.

> <u>Medical Professions</u>: Licensing requirements (medical licenses, especially for drug-related crimes) make it difficult for any felon to secure these jobs.

> <u>Child Care</u>: Jobs involving working with children, are off-limits to felons, particularly those convicted of sexual crimes (registrants).

There are other sites on the internet with more detailed information you can research, but the information listed here will answer some questions.

To Disclose or Not Disclose

When I was arrested, I thought everyone knew about me, but I avoided the feeling that I needed to tell people or offer details. In the county jail, I tried to keep a low profile, even though everyone in the cell block had been told my charges, thanks to one of the short-term residents with a subscription to the local paper.

Once in the prison system, I quickly learned that the prison grapevine was very effective. If someone asked me why I was in prison, I decided the person already knew and perhaps was hoping to give me a hard time if I denied what he thought he knew. So, my answer was simple. When asked, I would answer, "I am in prison for doing something I should never have done. My choices harmed not only my victims but countless other people affected by those choices. I am hoping that while I am here, I will learn how to do what it takes to change." I can't remember the exact words, and these words sound rather stiff, but you get the idea.

Despite being asked the "Why are you in here?" question many times, no one ever challenged what I said. One of my cellmates shared how he was molested as a boy and threatened to kill me, but I think he needed to confront me with anger, not action.

I share this background because when I started applying for jobs, I included the line, "You should know that I am on the state registry." In some cases, that was all it took for the interviewer to thank me for my time but say "No thanks" to my request for employment.

Withholding this admission is never a good idea. Background checks are required for most jobs; a prison sentence will stand out, and a sex offense will stand out even more. Disclosing up front might mean a rejection, but disclosure speaks to a desire for honesty.

Every job application you consider will put you face-to-face with the question of disclosure. Someone will find out sooner or later, so being transparent from the start is the best route.

The Micah Center

In the county in which I live, one of the homeless shelters also runs a separate resource service called *The Micah Center.* The prison aftercare network to which I belong frequently recommends this support site to anyone in reentry, but especially to registrants in reentry who are facing homelessness.

The Micah Center offers case management, computers and assistance in their use, a drop-in center (especially critical on cold Wisconsin days), a guest grant program (assists transition for both housing and employment for those who qualify), and on-site mental health/AODA services. Not all cities have a program as extensive as this, but it is worth asking if something similar exists in your area.

Additionally, this same homeless shelter offers a program called *The Joseph Project*. This is an extensive four-day employment training course that includes transportation to and from the training site. Businesses participating in *The Joseph Project* usually hire the individuals trained at their site.

Because these efforts are not widely advertised, it is considered worth your effort to ask if they are available to you when you seek help finding employment.

Jail/Prison Ministries

While they can sometimes be difficult to find, local ministries focused on reentry can be an excellent resource. Some maintain lists of companies willing to hire a formerly incarcerated person as well as registrants. It might seem strange to list registrants separately, but in most states, registrants face more complications and/or restrictions such as those already listed.

One point I think is important to mention is that most ministries will support reentry efforts *to the extent they are able*, but few will do the legwork for a registrant or anyone else in reentry. I have, for example, received letters asking me to provide as much contact information as I can for companies willing to hire registrants.

Some have suggested that I should call those companies for them, explain their situation, and ask if employment would be possible based on what I was able to share. Neither I nor the ministries I know work that way.

What ministries do is provide contact information for various services in their area. They will help in whatever way they can to make reentry as successful as possible, but, as I said, they won't do what a registrant can and should do. In my own reentry, it was such a blessing to talk with people willing to help because they listened without judgment. They weren't talking to Bob, the registrant. They were talking to Bob.

Workforce Development Centers

Over the years I have been involved in prison ministry, I have found that most cities either have a workforce development center, a job center, or are close to a city that does. These centers provide up-to-date information on job availability, resume preparation assistance, and other help most of us would never have thought we needed. An internet search for either workforce development or job centers will point you in the right direction. Don't forget to be as specific as you can (i.e., "job search" and <city>).

In most cases, because internet access is not permitted for registrants on parole without permission, agents will grant their clients permission to use job center computers if their time on the computer is supervised. I knew a man who got permission to do a supervised computer job search. He was monitored for part of the time, but was left on his own when the supervisor saw he was using the program correctly. Using the job search program correctly wasn't the issue. The issue is possible access to pornography on the internet.

At the next meeting with his parole agent, the man was asked about the job search. Specifically, he was asked if there was supervision the entire time. His honest reply was "no." The agent's response was to threaten to revoke his parole for violating his parole rules. That revocation didn't happen, but he told me later that he had learned his lesson.

If the job you are interested in requires a resume, both centers will work to help you create one. I often recommend that the first thing to do when entering a job center is approach the information desk and say, "I am on state parole and in reentry. Would someone be willing to help me?"

You won't be the first or the last to make such a request. In my over 30 years of experience in this ministry, I have never heard of anyone who was refused help. The people who work at these centers want you to have success – if you'll let them help.

I asked readers of *Into the Light*,
"Describe your efforts to find employment."

Right now, I am unemployed, but between you and me, I was never in a hurry to find a job. I feared that if I got a good job, I would lose my social security and not have that guaranteed money each month to pay my rent.

*****

I went out yesterday to check out some temporary employment services and to eat dinner. I found one temp agency and was told I needed ID. The woman who had come out to help me at this agency looked like she was afraid of me. I don't think it was self-consciousness or paranoia because I haven't felt that way about others.

I also called my old boss [from before prison days]. I told him that if any potential employer calls him, he should just be honest about why I left and explain it in a way that will be advantageous to all. This application did not ask about incarceration, but how can I honestly explain the lapse of employment for the past 4.5 years? Even Christian friends suggest I lie, but I'm doing what I know is right and let God get all the glory.

*****

Still working on that issue, as my age is a primary factor in obtaining employment. There are employment opportunities within my living area; however, they are skeptical about employing someone my age.

***

At first, it was strange, because there are no more paper applications. Applying for a job is mostly done online, which was a big change and challenge for me because of the very limited use of computers at the halfway house. Getting my first job, I just happened to be in the right place at the right time. A manager of a hot wings place was in the halfway house and recognized me from prison.

The job I now have came from an online application at a grocery store. I was interviewed and luckily passed the background check. Many factors helped me. My crime was federal, and most companies only do a local background check. Federal checks are more costly and, I think, considered a burden, so some businesses don't do them. I got a 10-year sentence and served 7 ½ years. So, on the application, I could truthfully say I had not been convicted of a crime in the past seven years.

I urge all of you to apply for work as soon as you can, because it takes the state a while to issue you a level for SORB. Until that happens, you are in limbo as far as your information being out there. Because I applied early, they did not find me on the SORB (registry). Apply and make yourself available for as much work as is allowed, and then work like you're making up for all that lost time. Employers love a good work ethic.

***

In my second month out, I found employment at a local bar and grill - cleaning, cooking, and doing whatever the owner asked me to do. After three years working here, I finally got a better-paying job at a warehouse where I have now been for three years.

***

I had some difficulties finding a job with my SO label, but I found work within a week.

***

Finding jobs depends on your willingness to look for one and your level of honesty. It's better to disclose that you were in prison than trying to hide that information. They will still find out.

A Place to Work

I was fortunate that the friend I live with was a welder and knew his employer was looking for workers for various jobs. I have been blessed to have been hired full-time within 30 days of my release. I've been with the company for two years now and have learned to do a lot of jobs.

* * *

Employment wasn't a problem because I'm retired. Most people released from a Sex Offender Treatment Program have a hard time in this state finding a job.

"What Do You Ask of God?" (ITL)

Some days were good days for the blind man as he sat among the beggars just outside of Jericho. Other days were not. This day, however, his life would be changed, for Jesus of Nazareth was coming down the road.

The blind man called out, "Jesus, Son of David, have mercy on me!" Those near him told him to be quiet, but he called out all the louder, "JESUS, SON OF DAVID, HAVE MERCY ON ME!" Jesus stopped and said, "Call him."

So, they called to the blind man, "Cheer up! Get on your feet! He's calling you." The man threw aside his cloak, jumped to his feet, and came to Jesus.

"What do you want me to do for you?" Jesus asked him.

The blind man said, "Rabbi, I want to see."

"Go, your faith has healed you." Immediately he received his sight and followed Jesus along the road.

Based on Mark 10:46-52

We aren't told whether the man was born blind, but in the days of Christ, most blind people earned their living by begging. No one offered them a cure, a return of their sight, just a place to sit in designated areas where those who felt so inclined might show pity and toss a few coins. I can just about hear the words even now, "You were *born* blind—probably a sin of your parents."

"There is no known 'cure' for sexual deviancy at this time." So reads the first of a list of concepts that form the foundation of one state's treatment program for sexual offenders. How would that statement balance with "There is no known 'cure' for blindness at this time." I would pray that in the first sentence, the words *at this time* might convey a desire for a time when maybe there *would* be.

The blind man would have remained blind had he not persisted, had he not demanded to be heard. Jesus called to him, and he threw aside his cloak, perhaps fearing that he might trip because of it. His faith drove him forward, the desire of his heart—to be able to see as others saw—acting like a magnet.

Jesus didn't immediately say the healing words the man expected to hear, but instead asked what the blind man wanted him to do. The blind man simply said, "I want to see."

Maybe I am looking at this the wrong way. Maybe the statement "There is no known 'cure' for sexual deviancy at this time" is really the state acknowledging the sin and not the sinner. Somehow, I doubt that. Sin and sinner become interchangeable in most prison settings.

Before some of you get the idea that I am advocating the elimination of state-run treatment programs altogether, I will assure you that I am not. In my own group treatment, I came face-to-face with parts of myself that I had never faced with honesty before. I saw my selfishness, my misguided lust, and my ignorance exposed.

But because of the faith-based balance offered in Bible studies and chapel activities, I also saw that not all that was within me was evil. I came to believe with all my heart that Jesus was asking me, "What do you want me to do for you?"

"Make this all go away."

Instead of answering the way I wanted, Jesus touched my heart and brought to life the words "And look, I am with you always; yes, to the end of time" (Matthew 28:20).

After the blind man received his sight, those who knew him didn't refer to him as Bartimaeus, the blind man. More likely, they referred to him as Bartimaeus, the man who was once blind but now could see. And it is highly probable that Bartimaeus himself would never forget that he had been a blind beggar. Scripture does tell us, however, that he followed Jesus along the road.

Being able to see was not the end for the man, but the beginning. Perhaps others excused some of the man's past attitudes because of his blindness. Having received his sight, those attitudes would have to change. Whereas before, his workday consisted of sitting among the beggars, now he would need to find some other means of supporting himself. We aren't told how he would do these things because the story's focus was on the mercy and love of Jesus. But the fact remains, the blind man met Jesus and was blind no more.

At some point in my own treatment, I finally accepted the truth that I had molested and had done great harm. Scraping away the layers of denial is never an easy or painless thing to do, and when that truth hit me in the face, I was devastated. I felt the millstone around my neck and the weight of despair pulling me down. But that's not where God wanted me to remain. God wanted me to experience the redemption won on my behalf through the death of Jesus on the cross.

What a miracle! What incredible joy I felt in knowing and believing that my sins had been forgiven! I was still in prison. I still had group meetings, wore prison clothing, and felt the forced physical isolation from those I loved. Yet it *was* different.

God did not strip away the difficulties of prison life. He didn't make my return home free of tension, nor did he place everything I wanted in my lap as time passed. He simply reminded me that he *was* with me in ALL things.

If a system of treatment proclaims, "Once a sex offender, always a sex offender," it falls far short of what it could do for those desiring a new life. Such a system will find itself unable to reach beyond its own human limitations. So, what, then, is the answer?

In my humble opinion, nothing speaks truth louder than the truth of consistency, the truth of living in the way one is meant to live, day after day, year after year. The state does not have to prove itself. I must prove myself. So do you. The question now remains, "What is it that you ask of God?"

Part Five

Meeting Basic Needs: A Church
Connection

9

A Place to Worship

I started this chapter by searching the internet for suggestions that might be helpful. I typed "Finding a church for a sex offender," and started the search. Normally, I cringe at the use of the term sex offender because it is inaccurate unless one is constantly reoffending. Most states use "registrant" as a more accurate description, although I don't think the word has found traction in the public's daily usage.

As the results began displaying, I noticed that only a handful could be considered helpful. Unfortunately, they didn't offer any suggestions or steps on finding a church family. Instead, they offered comments about why registrants *should* be allowed to attend church services. So, if my search hadn't produced the kind of advice I was looking for, what were the answers I was being offered?

"What to do if a sex offender seeks membership?"

"How to protect your church family from sex offenders."

"Church Liability and Registered Sex Offenders."

In short, the results were either heavy on supporting "No Admittance" policies or establishing "This is what you can and cannot do" guidelines for registrants who might be allowed on church property. Most entries were dated ten or more years ago – as though the standards set then didn't need any current updates, since I saw noting recent.

WHY BOTHER WITH CHURCH?

While in prison, I was in the chapel whenever I had the chance. It was where I was spiritually fed, where I was offered hope, and where I learned I was still part of the Body of Christ. Whenever I returned from any chapel activity, I signed the request for participation form for the next opportunity.

After a few weeks of regular chapel attendance, the unit sergeant would sometimes call out, "Van Domelen, are you going to Bible study this morning?" Whatever I was doing was set aside, and, as I signed out, I took the opportunity to thank that man. Every now and then, he smiled in response.

Before I was arrested, I had never given up on God, although I often thought I had given God enough reason to abandon me. My arrest was, I knew, the answer to my prayers for freedom from the dark and harmful choices I made and the addiction I hated but couldn't stop.

Attending chapel was not meant to be for dealing with the issues that brought me to prison. Chapel time was meant for connecting with God, for asking forgiveness, and for letting his love touch parts of my heart so deeply wounded. The more I surrendered myself to God, the more I began to see a separation between what I had done and who I was meant to be. That is a simple yet powerful concept. No, it's more than simple. It's profound.

Chapel vs Church

Prison chapels are not perfect, nor are all those who attend Bible study or chapel services sincere in the reasons for attending. Cramped into a 6x8-foot cell, any opportunity to get out can be appealing. For some, chapel was also a place to meet friends or play a game where they could monopolize the time with long, drawn-out testimonies that were more show than substance.

Aside from the misuse of chapel offerings, there were those who attended with hearts drawn to reconnecting with God and those who wanted to learn more about God. For them, chapel was an invitation to feel God's love, to know of his forgiveness, and to grow in their appetite for all things related to God.

As I shared earlier, prison chapels are not perfect, but a bonus for me was the absence of loud profanity and posturing as proof of toughness.

One day, as I returned from the chapel, a guard shared with me, "When you guys come back from chapel, the unit is different.

It's quieter, and my job is much easier."

Maybe some would disagree with me, but I think after spending an hour or so thinking and sharing about God, we brought the Holy Spirit back to our unit, a spirit of peace and calm.

What I will share with you now is not something everyone experiences, but I know that I did.

By the time I was released, chapel services had become events I both enjoyed and looked forward to. Sometimes, the presence of God quickened in those around me, and we worshiped as a body, not as individuals keeping to ourselves. In short, chapel was a time of sharing as a faith community.

When I was granted parole and the time for returning home drew near, I began to think about returning to the church I had attended for so many years. I started to imagine worshiping in the new way I had learned in prison chapels. And I suspect I thought church would be just like chapel – except for the absence of guards.

I had anticipated some awkwardness, knowing that these were the people whose trust I had betrayed and whose lives I had harmed. But I held on to the idea that I was once again part of this faith community. We would be worshiping together.

In the chapel, most of us connected with each other, sang with full voices, and listened intently to God's word. In my home church, I couldn't feel that same connection. Instead, several hundred people occupied pew space, stood and sat at the appropriate times, and, if there was singing, it sounded weak and unenthusiastic.

It was the singing that saddened me the most, because I believe God takes great joy in us when we lift our voices in praise. With the occasional exception, however, church was seen as a requirement by those in attendance. I sometimes thought they were saying, "I might have to be here, but no one can make me participate." And those who felt that way didn't.

In the 37 years since my release, I have come to understand that my expectations for worship were mine, and not everyone's. I had no right to tell anyone what I thought they should do, or how they should sing or pray. What I could do, however, was worship God as I felt led to worship God. If someone noticed and felt encouraged, then that would be my witness.

I can't say what you will find in the church you attend. I can only share from my experience a frustration that was legitimate for me. I still wish for a more united, participatory worshiping church, but I pray that it becomes a reality in God's timing. If you find yourself attending a church that truly worships, thank God and sing praise!

10

Finding a Church

THE CHURCH YOU LEFT BEHIND

It might be awkward for you, but you can start preparing to become part of a faith community even while still inside. As I shared earlier, it was my hope from the start to return to the church I attended before my arrest.

About a year before my release, I asked my wife to talk with our pastor about my return. Knowing it was my responsibility, I also wrote him a letter, sharing some of what I thought were the changes expected of me, changes that I believed took place while in prison. The purpose of doing this was to open the door of communication. I really wanted to know where I stood as a member of this congregation, information one cannot get without asking.

I was fortunate that the result of this communication was the pastor's approval for me to attend. It might have been tentative or even "I wish he wouldn't," but my request was approved.

His decision didn't mean that the whole congregation would be notified, nor did it mean there would be any kind of welcome mat. As a matter of fact, at the close of my first service since returning, only a few close friends approached to wish me well. Some wanted to know how I was doing, while others wanted to express their anger over my betrayal.

As difficult as it was to hear that anger, I needed to know how they felt because it took courage for them to share that. It also took a little courage for me to accept their anger without wanting to cut them off or minimize some of what they were saying.

It would have been easy for me to come back at them with "You don't know all the therapy I have been through, all the challenges I have faced." But that would have made the conversation go the way *I wanted it to go.* They didn't deserve to have their feelings slapped down, and I certainly didn't want that, either.

THE DENOMINATION YOU LEFT BEHIND

Based on the letters I receive, many of you shared a heartfelt connection with the denominational church you grew up in. Some of you might still have the same connection I did with your home church, so the communication I mentioned earlier is an important step in reentry. But some of you had already been told you would not be welcome.

Being rejected by your home church is not necessarily a rejection by the entire denomination. Some cities, like mine, have more than one church of the same denomination within city limits, so if you are willing, there are things you can do.

If you are returning to the city where you formerly lived or near that city, you can write to the city's Chamber of Commerce. While this might not always work, I have heard from registrants who wrote, and they said it did.

Chamber of Commerce
Local Church Directory
City, State, Zipcode

In a brief letter, they shared that they would be moving to the area and wanted information about x-denominational churches. If I were writing that letter, I wouldn't go into a long explanation of why you aren't using the internet, but would simply say, "I don't have internet access." Or you could say, "I will be in reentry soon and hope to connect with a church of x-denomination."

One man told me that he used this system and received a printout of all the Methodist churches in the city where he hoped to live. It's worth a try.

Perhaps the most difficult part of finding a church willing to be supportive of your return is coming to the realization that many churches don't want you around. You might want to respond with

"But aren't you a Christian? Would Jesus reject me the way you are rejecting me?" Don't.

You might hear nothing but silence in response to your questions. You might see people turn and walk away. You might even hear yourself raising your voice with some profanity thrown in and sounding like the guys in the day room trying to be tougher than anyone else. The only thing your outburst will prove is that you are no better than the language you use, and you will have justified their rejection.

At the very least, I have found most Christians want a sign of repentance, although they might not know what that looks like when faced with a registrant. For most of their lives, they have heard "Repent of your sins," and that's what they expect you to do. Like many life-changing things, repentance is a process.

REPENTANCE IS CONFUSING

The wheels of the legal system moved very slowly from the time of my arrest through the court procedural hearings and to my actual sentencing date. In my case, it was 13 months from start to finish. In those 13 months, I had already begun to change.

For weeks and maybe months, I saw most things through the lenses of "What's going to happen to me?" or "Why can't this all just go away?" Eventually, I saw past myself and began to understand the harm that I had caused. The trust I had betrayed. The wounds that might never heal for some.

One weekend, my wife and I were invited to a rummage sale being held by a family very close to us. In case we wondered, it was made clear that we *were* being invited, so we accepted.

Other than greeting our friends, I remember looking at things for sale but being very quiet, not at all outgoing. As we prepared to leave, we came face to face with our pastor. The silence between us was awkward.

Finally, I smiled and asked how he was. I didn't know it, but that was the wrong thing to say. Later, I learned that he was very angry that I was even there. He was angry because I smiled when talking to him. Most of all, he was angry because he felt I had offered no sign of repentance.

I thought about his response to me for days and wondered, "What exactly did he want me to do? Cry? Fall to my knees and beg forgiveness?" Maybe none of those things. Maybe all of them.

GENUINE SIGNS OF REPENTANCE

Because this is such a serious issue for anyone in reentry, I looked for something that might help define signs of repentance. I found that faith-based groups identified 8 to 12 specific traits as signs of true repentance. I offer this compiled list as an example of what others might expect of you, but I believe that God will make clear the direction you need to go.

As you read them, ask yourself how you feel about what you have just read. Then ask yourself if someone could identify that trait in you.

1. A repentant person takes responsibility for what he has done without making excuses or blaming someone else.
2. A repentant person experiences what is called a Godly sorrow, not because of the consequences that follow, but because the sin was an offense against God and therefore was an assault on that relationship with God.
3. A repentant person is willing to verbally confess his sin, both to God and to the person(s) sinned against. This confession is an act of humility.
4. A repentant person is willing to make amends for his actions, either with some restitution or a legitimate effort to restore relationships.
5. A repentant person is willing to accept the consequences of his actions.
6. A repentant person has a true desire for change of behavior and a commitment to avoid any similar behavior in the future.
7. A repentant person does not demand or assume forgiveness but actively seeks it by prayer to God for those affected. The timing of forgiveness, however, is never in his control.
8. As a result of true repentance, one might experience

feelings of joy and restoration, resulting in a renewed relationship with God.

I have come across people who will use a list like this to determine if a person has successfully repented or has failed to do so. Anything that doesn't look like the list is proof of an unrepentant heart, a heart that is not to be trusted.

When people say things like "He doesn't *look* repentant," I am confused because the things that really matter with us are often the hardest to see on the surface. On the other hand, a heart that agrees with the list makes choices based on that – not because the list demands that they do, but because a restored heart will choose to do them automatically.

Nothing Open

Sadly, sometimes the door remains closed despite sincere efforts, and membership applications are returned "Not Approved." I could understand how one facing so much rejection might be tempted to just give up. After all, church on the outside looks nothing like church on the inside, where reconciliation and restoration are the stuff of dreams.

But before you consider giving up, look at all you have been through on your journey to get to the point of life outside prison walls. I am pretty sure that when the doors of prison opened to receive you, you might have seen a sign that read, "Abandon all hope ye who enter here." If God brought you this far, why can't you believe that he will get you where you are meant to be? The schedule for restoration might be uncertain, but the church body, as confusing as it can sometimes be, is meant to be a part of that. Maybe they just don't know it yet.

Thoughts from Registrants

I asked readers of *Into the Light*,
"Describe finding a church to attend or
finding church support."

Finding a church was difficult in that some churches do not permit people with certain criminal backgrounds to attend their facility due to insurance stipulations or previous incidents relating to a person's history. Yet there are churches that will open up to us. Transparency is the key to succeeding even in an environment like this.

***

I was blessed by one of the Christian brothers from prison who had been in the same halfway house and had found a great church. I met one of the leaders of a recovery group there, and also with the pastor.

He introduced me as a friend, and they welcomed me with open arms and no questions. God had already planned it all out. That first day I met with them, the pastor was preaching from Acts 12, where Peter is jailed and about to be brought out before Herod. He is visited by an angel and freed.

I spoke to the pastor about how that applied and touched me, because I had just been released from prison four days prior. He didn't ask any questions about my crime. He just accepted me. I am very involved at my church and no questions.

***

I went to talk to the pastor of the church I had belonged to. With the care of my pastor, I was able to remain a member of the parish. That first meeting was not an easy thing for me because I shared everything with him, but it was well worth it. I had a place to worship.

***

I was sitting in the day room of the homeless shelter, and one Sunday, I heard a staff member yell out, "Church bus is here!" I went outside, and when I saw the driver, my first question was, "What denomination is the church?" I was skeptical because I had problems at the last church of that denomination.

To this day, however, I am so glad that I went because I found I had a lot in common with the pastor: both Marine Corps Veterans, same age, stationed at the same base, and knew some of the same former Marines.

***

I had a meeting with the pastor of the church I am currently attending. Since I am only intending to stay until September, the pastor said he would talk to some people, including the pastor of the church I will be attending in September.

The pastor has already discussed with me that it would be necessary for the leaders to know, but he doesn't feel it is good for the congregation to know. [Editor's note: *Exactly who to notify is a major issue for churches.*]

(Some months later) I also decided to meet with the leadership of the church I wanted to attend. God gave me the grace and courage I needed to speak, and the meeting went great. My pastor gave those present the opportunity to ask any questions they had or to share feelings they might have had about my offense. They accepted me as a member of the church, and I felt genuine acceptance from the people.

***

I was not interested in any church or church support.

Meeting Basic Needs: A Church Connection

***

I have probation officer restrictions. She isn't a believer, and that makes it difficult.

***

It was pretty hard. I contacted a church, but the pastor, who knew my family, never chose to talk more with me or write a letter of acceptance for me to come to his church.

"Have I Changed" (ITL)

HONEST ANSWERS

[36] "When they sin against you-for there is no one who does not sin-and you become angry with them and give them over to the enemy, who takes them captive to a land far away or near [37] and if they have a change of heart in the land where they are held captive, and repent and plead with you in the land of their captivity and say, 'We have sinned, we have done wrong and acted wickedly'; [38] and if they turn back to you with all their heart and soul in the land of their captivity where they were taken, and pray toward the land you gave their fathers, toward the city you have chosen and toward the temple I have built for your Name; [39] then from heaven, your dwelling place, hear their prayer and their pleas, and uphold their cause. And forgive your people, who have sinned against you.

2 Chronicles 6:36-39

I asked readers of *Into the Light* what I thought would be a fairly important question: "If someone knowing you before you were arrested asked, 'How would you say you have changed since your arrest?'" I asked the question for two reasons.

First, individuals convicted of child molestation face an uphill battle in terms of starting over. They must deal with the Sex Offender Registry and notification laws, communities not happy about their return, and the uncertainty of finding either a place to stay or to work. The task is made difficult because there is no one heralding the changes they have achieved in attitude or behavior choices because of the hard work they did in treatment programs.

Second, the job of rebuilding trust will only come after years of faithfulness to boundaries and evident growth patterns under the watchful eye of family, neighbors, and co-workers. I am convinced that unless individuals can recognize change in themselves, they will not have the confidence to stand with conviction in any setting.

So, this edition of *Into the Light* will be different. Rather than writing on a theme, I am going to share with you what others sent me as their response to the question. There will be a temptation, I think, to want to *correct* some of the thinking, and I urge you not to do that. Rather, see each entry as a statement representing their here-and-now coming from the writer's self-observations.

I think people who knew me before my arrest were not all that comfortable with me. I was controlling, self-centered (big-headed, some would call it), and driven by something or someone. They weren't wrong, but I doubt that they would have ever suspected the sexual turmoil in my life.

Prison was a turning point in my life. Released sixteen years ago, starting over was one day at a time, but there was always someone willing to help when help was needed. I think that a lot of people who knew me before prison are still cautious about what I say and do, but that's okay. In fact, that's healthy for me because they are making me earn the trust and respect I used to take for granted. I don't think they see me as the egocentric-driven individual with big secrets anymore. And I also think some are willing to give me a chance.

***

One thing that *hasn't* changed is my personality. I'm still goofy and possess a spontaneous, dry wit that those around me still seem to enjoy. That's a big plus because I really like my personality. However, a lot has changed since that dreaded day, and all for the best. I am more cautious about my thoughts and actions that do not necessarily involve anything related to my crime. Frankly, back then, I didn't know how to say NO to people and ran myself ragged so I didn't have to deal with real issues. That showed in my putting up a front that made me seem okay to everyone else. Now I am much more honest with my frailties and wretchedness because the only way from where I was is up. I like myself now, and I like that. Besides, I have a loving Savior who is ever holding me with His right hand and will never leave me – ever.

***

I would say that I have in God the ability to make the right choices in life, and for the first time, I am able to admit to anyone that I have a problem and am willing to do anything to make sure I don't make the same mistakes.

***

Since my arrest, I have had over eleven years to think about the subject of my inappropriate behavior—especially through books and stories of survivors of child molestation, as well as some brave women who came to our prison to tell their story in person. When I think about the never-ending negative and harmful effects my actions have caused my victims, it now makes me physically ill.

***

I've been in prison for forty months and got three months to go. I will be home. First and foremost, my spiritual growth has changed. I try to walk in faith now. I care about myself and others and have a positive attitude. Everyone will say I've done a 180° and that will be wonderful. With God first, everything will change for the better.

***

I have finally been able to admit that what I did was wrong and caused permanent and lasting damage to my victims and my family. I am learning to be empathetic. I can now admit openly that I am at fault for what I did - it all came down to choices. I have stopped trying to run my own life. I have also realized that I could struggle for the rest of my life with thoughts and urges, but I now have the tools and the power in Christ through faith to make the right choices so that there are no more victims.

***

The big change for me was when I was, with God's help, able to break through the wall of denial and justifications and come face to face with the horror of the harm I had caused others. It was a long, painful process to let go of the lies and face the ugly truth about myself. I cannot undo what I have done. But I am determined to live my life from now on as a helper rather than a hurter, a giver rather than a taker, and to abound in love as the way to a closer relationship with God.

The consequences of my past are painfully real and lifelong. But not just for me. My past victims have painful life-long consequences as well. My life today is about doing what I can to promote healing, peace, and hope to those God puts me in contact with. That is how my life has changed.

***

My first change was living with fear. I had never really known fear before prison. I had several sources of help, but by far, it was leaning on Jesus that brought me through the first three years. Once I decided I wanted a lifelong partnership and meant it, I began to find myself trying to improve in other ways. It is a slow process with ups and downs, but I truly believe I am a better person, more filled with love, charity, and brotherhood than before.

***

If my parents were to interact with me and see me, they would see immediate changes. They would foremost see the physical—the loss of 150 pounds. I've been told that I "sound different" by those over the phone. The most dominant personality changes, I believe, would be my open-mindedness, listening ability, and assertiveness. I used to have the mindset that I knew everything and that no one could tell me anything. Rather than listen, I used to tune out, yell, argue, and God knows what else when I was being told something I didn't want to hear.

I also used to expect people to know what I wanted and needed, and when they didn't, I'd get mad and throw a fit. I couldn't express my feelings. Now I listen to what others have to say, keep an open mind for new ideas and instructions, and make my needs known and express how I feel, although I still struggle a lot with that last part. God has brought me a long way, and I can't wait to show others what God has done in me.

***

I can tell you that I have more empathy, and I am taking full responsibility for molesting. In the past, I blamed God and everyone else for my problems. Today, I am taking responsibility for what I did and all the harm, pain, and damage that I caused. I also have a closer walk with Christ and know that, for the most part, God doesn't do quick fixes. He wants me to depend on Him and lean on Him. I have also learned that if God fixed every problem right away, I might tend to start believing I didn't need God. I am now a stronger person than I was, and Christ has taught me a lot of valuable lessons. He gets all the praise and honor.

***

I've been in jail for 28 years now, doing a life sentence in PA. I was a young wise guy, getting into trouble and staying out late. I didn't listen to my parents. Coming to prison at a young age, doing a life sentence, I thought I was somebody special. I was into drugs, violence, didn't care about people, and didn't want to listen to anybody.

Now, 28 years later, most of the friends I knew are dead from drugs, etc. When I came to prison, it took me time to realize that I needed change in my life. I asked God to help me, and please put me on the path He wanted me on.

Well, here I am today, a lifer with passion, love for other brothers, programs, church at least three times a week, Holy Name Society, Lifer's Organization, Jaycees, and participating in a program to help new brothers coming into jail. I really can't waste my time because God's path has me really busy. I love each day and thank God so that I can continue to live with my positive attitude. It's God's way or no way, and I prefer God's way.

***

The greatest change that I've made is that I now recognize that my happiness and peace truly and only derive from making my wife happy and proud of me. My wife has brought healing to my life and reconciled my damaged relationship with God and organized religion.

I now believe and truly trust that my wife will do nothing to lead me astray and that everything she does is beneficial to my mental, emotional, and spiritual welfare. I have a covenant of accountability with her in which I route all my letters to others through her, so that she may have the opportunity to read the letters if she wants to do so. I am committed to 100% honesty and absolutely no hiding in my relationship with her.

*****

[A portion of a letter from the above writer's wife to him]
I am really pleased and excited about how we have been able to talk to each other. I really like the feelings we share when we are together. I really like the fact that our relationship is getting closer in all ways. You are really changing in so many ways, mostly for the best. Your letters, your way of even holding me, is more romantic and very tender. I really love the change in you, and I can't wait until we are back together.

*****

I think the biggest change is that I don't feel like a scared little kid inside anymore. I no longer have to be in charge to feel like a man. I accept the things I cannot control, try to find my Higher Power's message for me in conflict, and I am not angry all the time. I pray daily, and I have a pretty good relationship with God. I am now a humble man who isn't afraid to admit his mistakes, say that he is wrong, or if I don't know something, I need to ask for help.

*****

I no longer desire the evil or high that drugs/alcohol filled me with. That searching for happiness is a dead end. The only satisfying peace is when God calls me and makes me want to come to Him with open honesty.

"Have I Changed" (ITL)

***

For the first time in my life, I have been totally honest with God, myself, and my loved ones. For me, to look so closely at what I have done and how it is affecting the lives of so many has been the most painful and liberating experience I have had. My journey of healing and change is now a spiritual one with the Lord's grace and mercy to guide me. In return, I give Him my trust.

***

Since my arrest, I changed by going through all the sex offender treatment programs, finding and learning who I really am, learning how to change my negative thinking into positive thinking, learning how much damage my sexual assault did to my victims, and feeling the pain that I had put them through. Also, I have changed when I finally got in touch with my Higher Power and opened my mind, heart, and soul to Him and allowed Him to guide me through each and every day of my life.

***

I am willing to take responsibility for my molestation and the damage it did. I desire to form relationships based on mutual benefit and edification instead of "What's in it for me?" I don't sweat the small stuff nearly as much. I have put my total faith and trust in Christ instead of following the watered-down "feel-good" gospel being preached today. Though I still have struggles and temptations, I am no longer preoccupied with sex. I am far more focused on spiritual matters than on material ones. I am making progress on living as though God is the center of the universe and not me. And I am far more willing to admit when I am wrong and to do what is necessary to make things right.

***

In the last 11 years of my incarceration, I have grown a lot spiritually and emotionally. Through God's grace and mercy, I've grown closer to Him and have learned more about myself and my continued need for God in my life. Without God, I fail every time! I am more responsible and more dedicated to serving God and

75

living within His protection, relying on Him to meet every need. I am much more in tune with my feelings and am learning how to deal with them in appropriate and non-destructive ways. But I still have a long way to go.

***

The people who knew me before I was arrested have seen me rededicate my life to Jesus and grow closer to my heavenly Father. I am working on my master's degree in biblical studies and have become more concerned with people around me, whereas before I was self-centered and looked out for number one.

***

I have come to realize that what I have done is so bad that everyone should be mad at me. I should be going to hell for what I did, but I asked God to forgive me and to show mercy on me. I want to have the faith needed to continue changing my life, and I believe that God will give me His amazing grace. God knew I was far from perfect, so He sent His only Son to die for me.

***

I was riding down the road and saw a sign in front of a church that said, "Church for Anybody." That was me, and I have been there ever since. I called the pastor and told him of my past, and he said, "You will be welcome here."

Part Six

Finding Support

11

A Support System for You

One of the blessings throughout my time in prison was the presence of spiritual support and encouragement. The chaplains I met were outstanding people who gave of their time and shared what God looked like in their lives. Despite ever-present security restrictions, they continued to do whatever they could to be the witnesses God called them to be.

However, I know from the mail I get that not every chaplain is like what I just described, but given the pressure under which they serve, I believe most do what they can.

Outside Ministries on the Inside

One group of people who are truly unsung heroes are the mostly retired individuals who take time out of every week to come spend an hour or so with inmates who are willing to attend. I'm pretty sure that before their entrance into the meeting room, someone among them said, "Okay, everybody. Big smiles!" because they brought an air of happiness with them as they greeted us. For the next hour or so, we were not in prison.

I never told anyone about my background in music, but when I attended my first *Faith at Work* Bible study, I was shown to the piano and given a songbook that had lyrics and chords – no notes. The song titles were, I think, mostly from a Protestant hymnal, but, being Catholic, were almost completely unknown to me. "Don't worry," I was told. "You'll figure them out." And after a while, I did.

Inside the room with these people, I might have been an inmate, but to these volunteers, I was Bob, the guy who played piano. The presence of God that I felt in them and in their manner of teaching was a God of joy, a God who loved us all beyond our imagining, and a God who called us. The more they shared, the more I wanted to live with that presence of joy and love.

They also represented the outside world beyond the bars and the barbed wire fences, a world that we all knew lay ahead.

The Anti-Fraternization Policy

The men and women with *Faith at Work* gave us as much as they could, but the one thing they couldn't do was offer us connections with outside services, such as employment or housing. For those of you who might be awaiting your release and looking for help in this book, you might wonder why Joe, who leads Bible study, cannot set you up for a job interview. He can't because he is bound by the *anti-fraternization rule.*

Simply stated, this rule says that if someone does ministry *inside* prison walls (like the *Faith at Work* Bible study group), they are not allowed to participate in any prison ministry-related activities *outside* of the walls. For example, because I am sending *Into the Light* to people in confinement, I am not allowed to enter prisons to do ministry, such as leading a Bible study.

I know that sounds confusing and begs the question why, but the rule was established to protect individuals on both sides of the fence. It's not important to go into more discussion of this other than to say that if you are in confinement, don't ask those who come into prison to be part of your reentry process. You would be putting them at risk of being banned from doing the good work they do.[1]

Outside Ministries on the Outside

People involved with jail or prison ministries are among the most welcoming people I have ever met and continue to meet. They never asked, "What are you in for?" but instead, "How are you doing? Do you need some help with something?" And if I answered yes to needing help, we talked and decided the best way to get a solution.

What surprised me most was that those reaching out were

---

1   Anti-fraternization polices may vary in practice depending on the state and the institution.

willing to be alongside me in the process, but they would not do something I needed to do myself.

Occasionally, I receive a letter from someone approaching reentry who wants me to find them an apartment – usually within a given monthly rent range and in a specific part of the city where they want to live. I have also had requests from those approaching reentry to submit applications for employment on their behalf.

Recognizing personal responsibility is an important part of reentry. Looking for housing, finding a job, or connecting with a faith community is never easy under ideal circumstances. Being a registrant coming out of prison makes everything harder, but not impossible. Trust that God is part of the process.

MINISTRY RESOURCES

Prison Fellowship, Crossroads Prison Ministry, Celebrate Recovery, and Servants of Christ Prison Ministry are among the many faith-centered ministries serving those in reentry. But where do you find them?

If you are still inside:

- Start by asking the chaplain for contact information for a reentry ministry. Often, they know of organizations that have proven themselves in their service. They might not know anything, but you won't until you ask. The worst they can do is say, "No." But at least you will have asked.
- Ask volunteers who come in for Bible study. They can recommend ministries if they know of them, but you will have to find a way to connect.
- Ask any family members or friends if they would Google "Prison ministries near me?" or some similar search phrase.

If you are in reentry:
- Probation and parole officers sometimes know of reentry groups and may be able to give you directions in contacting a ministry, but not all are willing and may see such a request as not a part of their job.
- Homeless shelters are often familiar with reentry

support systems in the area for those coming out of prison.

- If you have contacted a church willing to support you, the pastor might also help you make a connection with a ministry or support group system. A church family is ideal, but even they might not be able to help you as a registrant.
- In many states, one may call 211 for a menu-driven list of support services available.

There is nothing that makes reentry more difficult than doing reentry with the mindset, "I can do this on my own." From my experience, those who think that way may be doing so out of a false sense of pride, or they may be going alone because they are fearful of someone finding out about their prison background. And for us registrants, that fear might be valid.

Maybe you managed to go through your time in prison as a loner, but it is more likely there was at least one person you came to trust, a person with whom you spoke openly about most things – or at least as much as you wanted to share with anyone.

Those 'friends' helped make the time pass. More importantly, if you had one, this was someone who would hear your fears and concerns and not make you feel stupid for having shared them.

I shared earlier that, while at a halfway house, I attended Milwaukee Area Technical College, where I hoped to get a degree in accounting.

Not long after I started there, it was suggested I might like to tutor students who were struggling with coursework. Because it was a way for me to earn money, I sought permission from the halfway house warden, got it, and added tutoring to my daily schedule.

There was a woman who coordinated the program for those of us who tutored others, a woman I found easy to trust. She knew I was in reentry because I had told her, so when I was granted parole, she was the first person I told at the school. She got up out of her chair and came toward me with a big smile and open arms. She was openly happy for me, and that made me feel great!

Thoughts from Registrants

I asked readers of *Into the Light*,
"What were your experiences finding a support system?"

I found no support through church. As I met more people and was able to get to know them and share my life and what I had chosen to do, I developed a small support group.

***

Support, strangely enough, came from group. It was comforting to sit down with the other "degenerates" and realize that, in spite of being the outcasts of society, we were actually a decent bunch that made some poor decisions.

***

My first parole agent asked me to attend a support group. I wasn't sure about it except that I said, at the beginning of all this mess, that I would do anything and everything to keep myself away from going back to prison. To this day, I continue to go to Circles of Support meetings weekly, and that is the best thing that helps me stay out.

***

Where I am, finding a support system has been people willing to help with everything from getting free clothes, food, warm showers, as well as offering me assistance with jobs, housing, and medical help. It's also volunteers coming in on a regular basis to help with meals, laundry, and cleaning.

Finding Support

***

My family and a few friends are my support system and are there for me any time I need to talk about anything.

***

No problem.

***

Finding support was not difficult at all. Several of my peers here [where he was staying] are ex-inmates and on the registry. Therefore, they know the ins and outs of what a new resident will face and are willing to assist them as much as possible. I feel I have a good support system in this community and really see the need for those coming out – sex offender or not – to establish a strong support system. They should also not be afraid to ask for help when needed, even if simply talking.

***

Church offers great loving support. We have breakfast for the homeless, addicts, and outcasts, where there is always so much love evident. You can find Celebrate Recovery and other groups to attend. Family is key, so be open and honest. Share and ask for help. Find a good group therapist for your required probation treatment. Being able to share is huge, and what others share will be so helpful. If others find out your charges, have a good and truthful explanation.

***

I am lucky to have a close friend who has stuck by me. It is great to have someone other than family who knows me, knows what I did, and how I have changed. It really helps to have someone to talk to or to get a bite and hang out.

At first, when I met up with him, it was a bit strained, but that has changed over time. I thought it would be awkward to go over to his house and hang out with his wife around, but she didn't ask anything or say anything. She just let me feel welcome. It was more awkward in my head than anything.

Also, my first wife is very supportive, and her husband is very

84

friendly and kind.

***

At first, it was difficult. People were skeptical of a newcomer in the neighborhood, and it felt like they were watching my every move. Yet, being open and honest with others and myself paid off. Now people accept me for who I am – not what I was or did.

***

My support group consists of five other guys released from the same program I was in. We have a chatline we participate in daily, where we encourage one another and share our life challenges. We also hold each other accountable.

Another support group for me is Sex Addicts Anonymous (SAA). I feel comfortable being around a group of guys who have the same issues as I, and I've made some close friendships there.

My family also supports me in my recovery journey. I am blessed to have a family that doesn't judge me, although they don't approve of what I did.

I have real friends, not my associates, but genuine friends, too. I also have female friends for probably the first time in my life.

"Those Who Hope" (ITL)

"... but those who hope in the Lord will renew their strength.
They will soar on wings like eagles;
they will run and not grow weary;
they will walk and not be faint."

Isaiah 40:31 NIV

*I*t Happened...

The house was quiet, almost a forced silence. My wife and children didn't know how they should respond to me, or what to say or do. So, for the kids, entering a room where I sat staring straight ahead was more than awkward. They turned and left.

The local paper had already announced my arrest, and our phone started ringing. Sometimes friends, sometimes not. My wife instructed our children to pick up the phone and ask, "Who's calling, please?" Friends would identify themselves. The others hung up.

Nothing was the same; despite my best efforts, I couldn't see the light at the end of the tunnel. It was all black, a blackness that I thought would define my future.

The Next Stage

The van deposited me and three others at the state's receiving center. I had my property in a bag. Some paper, a pen, a few stamped envelopes, a pocket *New Testament and Psalms* that was given to me by a member of the Gideons, and a Bible my wife purchased and had sent to me.

I was frightened, especially when I realized that my first cell ended up being in the segregation unit. I didn't know that there wasn't enough room on the receiving unit. I thought yelling laced with constant obscenities was just the way it was going to be. This was prison. This was my new home.

There was, however, a narrow window in that room, and I found I could open it about an inch. The smell of freshly cut grass came to me on a light breeze and filled my senses. And in that moment, I also felt God speaking to my heart, "*and now it begins.*"

A New Life
"We've decided to grant you a parole and hope that you won't make us regret that decision." I cried.

> *… but those who hope in the Lord*
> *will renew their strength.*

The hope that I could not find in the days following my arrest was brought to life little by little. It was nurtured by those willing to pray for me, and sometimes, just knowing that they were okay with being in the same space I occupied.

The hope was most certainly nurtured by my wife and family in ways not many in prison get to experience. I never took that support for granted, and even today, they are a foundation of love that allows and encourages me to grow.

I chose the three defining moments above to share with you, times when it was clear to me that change was happening. Like many of you, there have literally been thousands of moments when I knew God was working in my life, despite and maybe because of the environment of prison. The complete blackness I felt and saw in the beginning was never again complete. God's light overcame it.

The word 'renew' is important because it is part of a process that became clearer and more real as my relationship with the Lord grew. That growth came in prayer, worship, and spending time in His word, learning and listening. And it came in surrendering my life to God.

When I fall short in that connection, as I often do, something feels different in how I see life. It's less joyful and certainly less hopeful. After all, what I have done is same old, same old, so what's the point of fighting the old inner person? In moments like that, I sometimes tell myself I *can't* change. The blackness returns... but not really. At the end of the day, I refuse to believe that it is how my life must be.

Sitting in that chair years ago, I had no strength and no hope. By the time I was transferred from the county jail to a state prison, I felt stronger but uncertain, a little afraid but believing. And when it came, the Parole Board's decision didn't change the empty-looking canvas I was staring at in my mind, but I felt strong enough to start adding brush strokes that would create a new image, a new future. I knew God had reached into my life and was giving me the strength to believe that a future based on hope was possible.

… soar on wings like eagles …

The image of eagles' wings was used in the Old Testament to represent the Lord's strength and loving-kindness in delivering His covenant people. "You yourselves have seen what I did to Egypt, and how I carried you on eagles' wings and brought you to myself" (Exodus 19:4).

Being renewed and reliant on God, we can soar beyond our imagination as God uses us. We will do things beyond our self-imposed limitations, certainly beyond the old self and that former life of darkness, because God is the wind upon which we soar.

… run and not grow weary …

As much as I wouldn't mind having actual wings that would allow me to go wherever I wanted, I have feet, and they are firmly planted on the ground. I am also at a time in life when I very seldom, if ever, run. But if I push myself too hard, I do grow weary. Yet I am really talking about more than that.

"And let us run with perseverance the race marked out for us, fixing our eyes on Jesus." (Hebrews 12:1-2) This is not a 5K or 10K race, or even a standard marathon of slightly more than 26 miles. This is a race that lasts our lifetime. It never stops.

On my own, this all seems beyond impossible, especially if I am not to grow weary. I know that on my own, I will tire and probably want to give up. Remember, however, that this is not a race I run alone. None of us does. For when we fix our eyes on Jesus, we are running on His strength.

To put all this into the reality of what I have done and all the harm I brought on others, this race will be one of living from day to day, doing whatever I need to do to stay free of any return to my past choices. I need to say no when I need to say no. When I stumble in any way, I need to remind myself whose child I am and get up to continue the race.

Perhaps putting this even more practically, if you take a moment to think of how you felt before your arrest, at the time of your arrest, and everything that has happened since, you have already been through much more than you'd have imagined. And you are still moving forward, still running the race even when it doesn't always feel that victorious.

… walk and not be faint.

I have been out of prison for more than 30 years, and some might feel I have run the race or reached the finish line. But the truth is that every day seems to bring new challenges, and not all of them relate to my past offenses. I decided that the goal is not to demand freedom *from* all temptation but to seek God to help me make it *through* temptation.

Most of those who have written to me recently have received a prayer I say every day, several times a day. It goes like this:

O Jesus, I surrender myself to you,
Take care of everything!

If you are in the habit of saying the Lord's Prayer, you already say part of this prayer in the words: *thy will be done.* Everything doesn't mean some things or even just one thing; it means everything! And then, being as reliant upon God as I can be, I trust that *my* choices will come from the center of *His* response.

You'll get through all that you must get through. You will face both temptation and adversity. You will find people who want to support and encourage you, but you will also be confronted by those who will hate you and refuse to make the burden of reentry any less difficult than it is. You are *not* alone.

Trust the God who was present at your birth to be with you to the extent that you will allow His presence. And pray most sincerely for the grace to give Him your all. Have hope because that is a gift from God. You are His – you always have been.

Part Seven
Official Matters
Probation/Parole, Registry

12

Parole Agents & You

On December 8, 1988, I was granted parole. For most of the day, my head was filled with images – mostly of the past and the people, but also images of the future that were probably more fantasy than reality. Realistically, however, I didn't think anyone would be throwing me a "Welcome Home!" party.

The next day, the warden called me into his office and said he would let me know when my appointment with my first parole agent would be scheduled. I had not even given much thought to that, but as I would have no choice in the matter, the meeting would happen when it happened.

A week later, the warden stopped me just before I left for school and told me that my agent was holding back on our meeting for some reason. I remember the warden then telling me, "You are ready to be out and starting over, so when I call your agent today, I am going to tell him that if he isn't here in the next few days, I am letting you go without that meeting." I had not expected to hear these words, but maybe something would happen soon. It did.

That same afternoon, I came back from my classes and saw a man sitting in the visitor's room. I don't know what I expected, but the man I saw sitting there was wearing an Aussie outback hat. It was the first thing I noticed because I didn't expect it.

We spent the next 45 minutes going over a contract release form, where I was told what I could and couldn't do. After each of the 45 items, I was told to put my initials on the corresponding line. Finally, that part was done.

His face had been set in a stony look – no smiles or warmth, just an all-business look. I was told that I was expected to do everything he told me and to do nothing out of the ordinary without his permission first. It was safe to think he frightened me, but I know now that was his intent.

How it worked

At first, I met with my agent every week. He set the time and, unless I had a good reason to request a change, that was the time we met. However, he was respectful of the fact that I had classes I could not miss, so at the occasional times when a conflict existed, he was willing to make a change.

Some who write me say that when they show up for a meeting with their agent, they get asked, "Is everything going okay? Are you having any problems?" These men told me that after a time, a simple no meant the end of that meeting, a quick goodbye, and "I'll see you next time."

My agent would ask those questions, but he would follow them with "Any deviant thoughts this past week?" The first time he asked that of me, I didn't hesitate to offer a confident "no." A few weeks later, I gave him a timid "yes." Rather than pull out a form that would revoke me, he asked, "How did you handle them?" He wasn't out to get me. He wanted to help.

I decided that if he wasn't embarrassed to hear my answer, I wouldn't be embarrassed to talk openly about my concerns. What really helped was that he expected me to have occasional images that I should not be encouraging. More importantly, he believed that how I dealt with them was more important than having them. In short, temptation is not the issue. How one deals with temptation is.

I doubt that all agents would have responded to me as he did. And maybe some of you reading this would say, "Boy, were you lucky. All my agent does is look for ways to revoke me." But lucky or not, I listened to that man, showed him the respect he deserved, and tried to be 100% honest with him regardless of the questions.

For his part, I think he came to trust me. He encouraged me to be part of a support group even though its meetings were 60 miles away. That group was Broken Yoke Ministries.

With time, I saw an occasional smile on his face in response to something I said, and I felt honored by that. During his regular random visits to our home, I felt that he respected my wife because he went out of his way to be like a welcomed visitor to our home.

Not All Agents Smile

My first agent eventually moved on, and another took his place. The questions were pretty much the same, and so were my answers. In my ten years of parole, I had nine agents. The first lasted the longest.

At one meeting, I was told that I was going to be part of a new system that agents would be using with registrants. Part of what that meant was that instead of meeting with a single agent, there would be two. I was a little uneasy to see both agents on one side of the desk waiting for me to sit down, but this was the "new" way, and I had little choice.

Again, the usual questions. I don't think they were prepared for what I considered to be the honest answers I gave them. Maybe more so as I followed the answers I gave with my own questions for them.

My faith and growing relationship with God, Jesus, and the Holy Spirit entered the conversation at that first meeting. I think they might have been expecting words of manipulation or minimization from me, but they didn't come. At my next scheduled meeting, I had a new agent.

A Wonderful Story

There was a woman who sat at a desk just inside the entrance to the Probation and Parole Offices. Always friendly, she greeted me each week in a way that didn't feel like my being on parole was an excuse for her to be short or rude with me.

One week, she checked me off on her list, called my agent to say I was in the office, and said, "I'm Mike's mother. Not much time passes that he doesn't ask how you are doing. Would you be willing to say hello to him at your next appointment?" I was a bit off balance because I remembered her son as a hardworking baritone player in one of the bands I directed. Mike was not overly talented, but he was a sincere, likable student. I said, "Okay."

The following appointment, he was already waiting for me when I arrived. The fact that he smiled made a big difference, and I was able to smile back. He asked simple questions, and I gave him simple answers. I did, however, ask for his forgiveness – not as a direct victim of mine but as someone whose trust was shaken by a man he obviously looked up to.

I didn't see him again after that, but I felt blessed that his mother paved the way for him to see a flawed person, redeemable and not defined by what he had done. Thank you, Mike's mom!

Thoughts from Registrants

I asked readers of *Into the Light*,
"What were your experiences dealing with a parole officer?"

My first agent was quite nice and willing to work with me for the 90 days I spent at the TLP (transitional living program). I used those days trying to organize things to get moved to my home county (a requirement by Wisconsin state law). One thing that really helped me throughout my time on parole was being honest with my agent and following all the rules of society.

***

(Written in 2002) I may have mentioned that the treatment I am in does polygraphs as part of the treatment. I don't think I told you mine was up and coming—it came and went so fast.

I was nervous about it, mostly because of not wanting to say anything that would be self-incriminating. I told the technician doing the polygraph of my concern, and he understood. He said that I could say and write things in ways that would not incriminate myself. I did that and was totally honest in sharing my history.

The polygraph said that I was deceptive. I failed the test. My therapist said that he doubted I would pass anyway because of the extensive history I had. Undoubtedly, I probably have more victims or experiences that I haven't remembered, and that alone would cause me to fail the test.

After nine years of treatment and being as open as I was, I thought I would pass it, even with the doubt of my therapist. I feel like I am being suspected of being a liar. I could say I felt like a failure, too. I just now realized and admitted that. I shared these feelings with the group and got some good feedback.

***

I was discharged with no probation or parole time.

***

With most things, dealing with my PO was easy. When it came to matters of religion, however, it was a different matter.

***

I had three different agents over the year I was required to report. My first was very open, honest, and helpful. I found him willing to be understanding and willing to help. He was very surprised, however, at how easy a parolee I was and took note of how quickly I hit the ground running after 23 years of incarceration.

My second agent was more impersonal, always looking for a reason to justify a violation, though he was impressed by the fact that I had all I needed, as well as a 'host' who did not have any concerns about me.

I only had my third agent for one day, as I was discharged two days later. He was very friendly.

***

My agent is very professional and has worked with me as much as possible to meet at a time that works for both of us. She follows the guidelines and doesn't interfere if it's not needed. She does hold me to all the requirements. I think that the biggest thing is to be open, communicate, and follow what the agents say.

If you have a difficult agent, just try to bear with them. If they go overboard, check with your guidelines, and if they are not following them, it's okay to say, "I have complied with everything. Can we just work through these requirements/Pants set out in my terms? I am not being unreasonable." In terms of group, it seems like most of the officers want to help to some extent and not have to be bothered wasting time bothering you.

***

I didn't have a parole officer, and I'm grateful for that. The guys I know on parole are, I think, treated unfairly most of the time.

"Testing, Testing . . ." (ITL)

Test me, O Lord, and try me, examine my heart and my mind, for your love is ever before me, and I walk constantly in your truth. I do not sit with deceitful men, nor do I consort with hypocrites; I abhor the assembly of evildoers and refuse to sit with the wicked.

Psalm 26:2-5

Most of us have at least one memory of someone stepping up to a microphone and, after blowing vigorously at it several times, saying, "Testing, testing." The result was often an unexpected, ear-piercing screech of feedback, with the one testing the microphone leaping back as though attacked by it. We might have thought the experience a nuisance, but it did validate the notion that something might not be as it should be.

Not long ago, an inmate wrote me to say that he felt *Into the Light* had gone over to the other side, sounding more like people who persecute sex offenders than those who support sex offenders. His complaint confused me, and I wondered what it meant to have gone over to "the other side." Wasn't the other side where I wanted to be, a man who would not even consider abusing a child? Perhaps he was suggesting that I felt sex offenders only get what they have coming, but I just don't believe that to be a valid statement.

The following morning, I read the above verse and the words *Test me, O Lord, and try me, examine my heart and my mind* leaped off the page. Immediately, I asked myself, "Do I really ask God to do this in my life?"

Part of me was afraid God would bring something to light I had hidden even from myself. Part of me wondered if I really wanted more testing in my life, more need to surrender my will to the will of God. And part of me remembered how much I had once believed God's love for me depended on what I did for Him, and for a moment I was afraid that I would not measure up.

Then I thought of the man's letter, and I considered another point. For every person with a sex-related offense (and in some ways for every *sinner*), the consequences of abuse affect him on at least three levels:

1. living in the face of victims and societal response
2. living in the face of the person he is and is becoming
3. living in the face of the wounded child within himself.

At the very least, this is a difficult balancing act to maintain, and I doubt that anyone can make the three levels equal. There is a need, no, a responsibility to become accountable at each level, and some might feel that their own abuse as children explained and maybe even justified the offenses they committed. But this can never be.

Test me, O Lord, and try me, examine my heart and my
mind.

The child in me looks up, wondering who is saying those words. Not everything was as it should have been while I was growing up, but I cannot say that I lived in terror like some people I have met. However, things did happen during my growing-up years. Some things I chose, and some were chosen for me. Even then, I knew when something was good and when it wasn't, regardless of how the behavior was chosen. Even then, I knew God reached into my heart.

I do not sit with deceitful men, nor do I consort with
hypocrites; I abhor the assembly of evildoers and refuse to sit
with the wicked.

If I wanted a list of the ways in which I fell short as a young man and then as an adult who went on to abuse, this verse might do. I sat with deceitful men and felt most comfortable with others like me, hypocrites who showed one face to the respectable world and another in the shadows of lust.

In adult theaters and bookstores, I found my assembly of evildoers—places where the wicked gathered and drank their fill of the poison that clogged their moral veins and blurred their vision of righteousness.

I wanted to say, "I'm just looking around … won't be staying … certainly not interested in the things that attract *you*." But I'm sure some of those other men were saying the same as they looked at me. The one thing we all knew was that we would not tell on one another.

Test me, O Lord, and try me, examine my heart and my mind.

When it counted, I failed every test. The downward spiral of my desires could only have the result it did. Whether they wanted it or not, others were harmed: my family, my victims, and those who had placed their trust in me. Accountability then was just a word; an escape from detection became a main goal in life.

If you are keeping track, we have covered two of the three levels, and I have been covering them in reverse order. Living in the face of victims and societal response is something that is held over me, something over which I don't have much control. The world thinks in terms of punishment and protection—punishment for offenders and protection for all children from the likes of me. They set the rules, and the rules they set don't necessarily take my needs into account.

If I sometimes write in a manner that seems to agree with the attitudes of society, which are based on rules that provide little in the way of practical healing for offenders, it is because all the shouting in the world will not convince society to seek more balance. I do not agree with those who threaten the lives of molesters released again into society, nor do I agree with prison sentences that cover a lifetime and end in civil commitment.

There is only one manner of living for the man or woman who is a registrant, one form of accountability that balances the other two levels. I believe that a person must be accountable first and foremost to God, daily asking God to test and try, examining the heart and mind. This accountability is equally as valid for those in prison as for those who have been released.

I cannot sit with deceitful men and women, because my life must be transparent and free of hypocrisy. Adult bookstores and theaters promote the very darkness I can no longer enter. My speech must reflect the state of my heart. Psalm 139:24 says,

> *See if there is any offensive way in me,*
> *and lead me in the way everlasting.*

In other words, "Lead me in *your* ways, O Lord."

Why is it that we fear having our "offensive way" exposed if it is something that makes life less than what it could be? I am no paragon of virtue, no walking saint free of sin, yet there are moments when I "know because I know" that I need to grieve those parts of me that are not of God.

At the same time, as accountability to God increases, He opens my memory to my childhood, fixing what was broken, or otherwise giving me an understanding of what happened so that I am not crippled by the memory.

Finally, as accountability to God increases, I can deal with the world and with the people to whom I must be accountable, knowing that my freedom really does depend in large part on how honest I am with myself and with God. The man the world sees in me must "walk the talk," for the talk is God's love.

"Testing … testing" was the voice I heard. "Here I am, Lord," I answered. "What do you want to know?"

13

The Registry

When I got out in 1988, I was told I needed to report to the local police station. I remember standing just inside the main entrance at a bulletproof window with a small, vented opening used for communicating. While waiting for someone to notice I was there, I started to feel a bit awkward, because all I could think was, "What am I supposed to say?"

This was one of those God moments because a man in uniform came to the window and asked, "How can I help you today?" Without hesitation, I answered, "I am here to register." Nothing more than that, but that was all that was needed.

Escorted into a small room, I was given a form, told to read it, and sign it. Then I was told to stand in front of a wall as my picture was taken, in the same way it was taken at the time of my arrest. This time, however, I had to hold a card with my state prison ID number written on it. After the set of pictures was taken, I was thanked and escorted to the exit.

I quickly learned that the police department just wanted to know where I was living and that I was following the contract I signed just before my release. Probation and Parole held me accountable for that contract, a list of 45 items stipulating what I could and could not do. Revocation was the price I had to pay if I failed.

But all of this was not the registry as we know it today. That registry did not yet exist. It does now.

The Registry

WISCONSIN 1997

On June 1, 1997, Wisconsin Act 440, entitled "Sex Offender Registration and Community Notification Law," became effective. This is Wisconsin's version of "Megan's Law," known nationally as a law intended to help protect society by identifying convicted sex offenders and their placement within communities. This law applies to all people who, <u>on or after 12/25/93</u>, were sentenced, in an institutional setting, discharged, or on field supervision for sexual crimes. [Source: "Eagle River Police Online"]

In the early days, there really wasn't much difference between Probation and Parole and Wisconsin's Sex Offender Registry. Beginning in 2000, I received a form that I filled out and returned within the required ten days, though I didn't think I would have been in trouble if I had mailed it back within a reasonable amount of time after the deadline. But why take a chance?

The information required was basic: mailing address, employment, educational situation, and vehicle registration. I learned quickly that every box had to be checked. Failure to do so resulted in the form being returned as incomplete. In recent years, they have requested a list of online accounts regularly visited, along with one's login identification. Passwords are not requested.

From the beginning, I have saved every document received from Wisconsin's DOC, registry-related or not. I have the option now to do the annual information filing using the internet, but I am leery that proof of submission could become more difficult if not completely out of my control. Whether you follow my example or not is your choice, but I know others who feel as I do.

In 2005, the State of Wisconsin passed legislation approving a $50 annual fee for anyone with sex-related offenses to partially offset the cost of being on their internet registry. Two years later, the annual fee charged was raised to $100. Several states have no fees, while others charge lower fees. I received a notice that I would be required to pay the $100 fee beginning in 2008, and I continue to pay that amount.

REGISTRY NITTY-GRITTY

When making notes for this chapter, I researched materials found on the Wisconsin State Legislature's website. I have never been one to feel comfortable with the way legislative information is written, although I am guessing that it is written to avoid misunderstandings. To be honest, I usually give up when I start to feel bogged down. Trust me, bogged down doesn't begin to describe it.

The section on what it costs a registrant to be on the state's online registry, for example, should have been easy to find. But it took a lot of scrolling through paragraphs and subsections before I finally found what I was looking for.

I found what I was looking for on the internet, and some would say care should be taken with the information offered. These days, the first answer to a request for information is answered by artificial intelligence (AI). In defense of the system, there are lots of links to other websites offering the information. After visiting some of them, I was satisfied that the AI information could be considered accurate for the questions I was asking.

Nitty-gritty is how I describe the requirements registrants must observe because several of them vary based on where one lives. For example, some who share with me say they must report in person to update their registry information quarterly. In Wisconsin, I fill out the form they send, and a month or so later, I get a notice to pay the $100 annual fee. No contact required.

Periodically, I am required to report in person to have my photo updated. I struggle a bit with that, not because I don't want my photo taken, but because I must hold a cardboard sign with my institution identification number printed on it.

The person taking my picture always listens patiently as I make the point that I committed sex offenses almost 40 years ago. While I admit to those charges, I am not planning to commit another offense. The number I must hold almost shouts, "You are the SAME man you were the date of your arrest! This is YOUR number. THIS is who you are!" Fortunately, the staff member doing her job agrees but reminds me that she has no alternatives to offer me.

A simple point I want to make here: You will meet many

professionals who do care about you and want you to have success. Don't label these people as "the enemy." The photographer in the story I just shared was one of the good ones.

I can't answer all the questions I get from those in reentry, because I don't know the answers, but I do point them to sources of information. Sometimes, that source is a parole agent. Though most agents are overworked and have larger caseloads than they should have, most will point you in the right direction. If you have an agent unwilling to help, ask around. Someone has the answer.

A LITTLE BASIC REGISTRY HISTORY

"One thing the registry should never be used for," Sarah Wescott said, "is to make life harder for sex offenders who may be working hard to better their communities and not reoffend." Wescott is the corrections services supervisor for the Wisconsin Department of Corrections and manages the registry with other DOC staff.

"It's a tool for you," Wescott said. "It's not something to be used to make the registrant pay again or harass them to leave your town. That's not the intended use."

Source: kenoshanews.com – 11/28/20

When I first read this, all I could think was, "What happened?" When first proposed, the registry was *"intended to help protect society by identifying convicted sex offenders and their placement within communities."*

Under Megan's Law, the State of Wisconsin wanted to know where I lived and worked. The Adam Walsh Child Protection and Safety Act of 2006 helped establish a national registry to track offenders and strengthen penalties for crimes against children. This registry, known as the Sexual Offender Registration and Notification Act (SORNA), has unified state and territorial registries into a single searchable database.

For many people, knowing where a registrant lived wasn't as important as having the power *to determine* where a registrant *could* live. Out of this desire to protect children, communities created residency restriction laws, normally 1500-2000 feet from schools, parks, or places where children normally congregate.

If you are moving into an area, you can get this information from the Probation & Parole office. The website for the community will also list requirements, but it can be difficult sometimes to wade through those sites in search of them. A shortcut would be to call the city hall and just ask. "I'm moving to <city> and want to know if there are residency restrictions for sex offenders." You might get asked if the question is for your sake, and if it is, simply say "Yes."

Not all communities have a specific distance from a location that children frequent. Instead, some communities rely on "No Loitering" laws. In short, you can't sit on a bench near the local swimming pool just because you want to do so.

My experience is that if I have a purpose for being in an area (i.e., a library), I am not violating any community laws. The easiest way to say this is to suggest that _you_ know why you are in a location for a given amount of time, and _you_ know what your real intention is. The most important boundaries that exist are those that we create for ourselves. Set them. Believe and live by them.

A New Home

When my wife and I decided to move closer to family, she used a quarter piece that closely resembled the size of the scale used on a map to determine if a possible address would be in a permitted area. As we got closer to making a choice, we contacted the local police department and asked whether the address would be appropriate.

We did find a home that fit our needs and budget that was approved for the area we had chosen, but something happened that we did not expect.

Not long after we had moved in, there was an unsigned envelope in our mailbox. It was a notification to the neighborhood that a sex offender had moved into the area with my name and address. That evening, I watched as cars came into our court, slowed down as they passed, and then slowed down again on their way out of the court.

One of our neighbors knocked on our door. Waving the envelope in my face, he said, "My daughters came home from school and found this in our box. They're scared! What am I supposed to do?"

I admitted to being on the state registry and that I had been since the registry in Wisconsin began.

"When were you arrested?"

"In 1985," was my answer.

Then he said something that surprised me.

"I have seen you in church and know that you are a Catholic. So am I. What kind of faith do I have if I don't try to give you a chance to move on? But I'll be watching."

Earlier that same day, he had crossed the street with his snowblower and shoveled our driveway. So, I asked, "If you had known then what you know now, would you have shoveled my driveway?" It took only a moment, but he said, "Yes."

I am not suggesting that you will meet with the same response as I got from that neighbor (and another who also stopped by that night), but I do believe God gave me the grace to be humble in the face of my neighbor's honest concerns. Nor am I suggesting that all Catholics would have done the same. This one did.

We have lived in this home for almost 18 years now. Our relationships with all our neighbors are polite but perhaps cautiously so. Every now and then, the neighbor part of the story above will see me working on something in the yard and ask if I could use some help. I don't turn him down.

Help! I'm on the Registry!

Some would describe the registry as an idea meant to protect, but it has become much more than that. The word itself has a life unto itself. Saying "I'm on the registry" will most certainly change relationships. It might get me rejected from an activity (even a faith-based one) or, worse, in some areas, get me asked to leave the church I might be attending.

Was that the intention of those who sought a way to honestly protect their children from possible molestation? There might be some reading this who angrily announce they would never harm another child. Maybe they won't, but there are individuals in reentry who don't think the same way. Sadly, a few actually look forward to abusing another child.

Some have addictions that are so intense that they feel they have no other choice but to have sex with a minor. Some believe they have their sexual drive (or whatever triggers their behaviors) under control. Their resolve melts under pressure, little more than a feeble defense system. So yes, I do believe some will reoffend, and yes, I do believe that the public needs to be watchful of them. That is, I think, the original intent of the registry.

As I described earlier, registrants face issues, sometimes major ones, when people learn they are on a state registry for those who have molested. Employment is more difficult to find than without that connection, and housing is more of an issue. In fact, in some parts of the country, if you live next to a parking meter, you have to list the meter number as an address to the authorities. Any change of location must be reported, even if it is an underpass.

My release from prison came at a time when this kind of registry didn't exist. Permission from the local police department and probation/parole office was needed to live in most cities. Employment applications included the question, "Have you been convicted of a felony?" followed by a request for more information.

By 2024, most states had removed this question because of a national "Ban-the-Box" movement. When I filled out application forms, I cringed a bit but answered the questions. My logic at the time remains the same today: What I did to be charged with a felony is a matter of public record, so why try to conceal it? I was turned down for several jobs, but eventually I found employment.

I would not be honest if I said I was never afraid of what someone might do knowing my background. Something happened to me not long ago that I hope will help you.

Scams can and do happen.

My wife and I were at a friend's home one evening when I got a phone call. "This is Sgt. Smith [name changed]. We sent you a notice last month to inform you that your placement on the state registry was being reconsidered, given the years you have been out without offense. That notice included the date and time of your court hearing. You chose to ignore that summons, and the judge issued a bench warrant for your arrest."

He went on to tell me that the police would be arresting me the following morning, but he also offered an option.

"I can," he said, "put a stay on the arrest if you are able to post a bond by noon tomorrow."

"How much?" was all I could say.

"Usually, the bond in situations like yours would be 10%. That comes to $3450. I will send instructions for you in an email and expect you to follow them."

Sure enough, within minutes, a PDF appeared in my inbox listing everything he had told me. It was on official stationery from the county sheriff's office, but I was in no state to question it. At the bottom of the page was a notice stating that the Bitcoin ATM machine at the sheriff's office was out of order and offering the address of two alternative sites.

The next morning, I went to the bank and withdrew $3450, then went to one of the addresses listed, where I slipped one $100 bill after another into a machine that eventually spit out a notice that the funds had been transferred to the identification numbers I entered.

The instructions told me to report to Sgt. Smith's office at the Sheriff's Office. All I had to do, he said, was meet him in the lobby because I just had to sign a form.

By this time, it was slowly entering my mind that I had just done something I would regret. Proof of this was the fact that I got lost driving to the Sheriff's Office not once, but twice – adding almost 35 miles to the trip.

When I finally arrived, Sgt. Smith was not to be seen, but I noticed a woman sitting at the reception desk. I asked for Sgt. Smith and was told there was no Sgt. Smith. She looked at me and said, "Oh, honey, you didn't give him money, did you?"

"$3450" was all I managed to say.

There is more to this story, but I think you get the picture. I heard that some registrants had been scammed, but I thought I was too smart, too knowledgeable about such things. I even warned others to be careful.

In the end, "Sgt. Smith" had waved the "Get off the Registry" card in my face, and I could get behind that. When I called the Registry office in Madison and explained what happened, I was told that there was a notice on the DOC website cautioning registrants about these scams. I asked the logical question, "If a registrant is not allowed to be on the internet, how is he supposed to get your caution?"

"The Parole officer should make sure their clients know," was her answer.

Really?

Before closing the conversation, I mentioned the bait offered to me as part of the scam. "You are *never* getting off the registry," were the final words before I hung up.

My wife and I live within a tight budget and try to avoid wasting money, so $3450 was quite a hit. She knew something was off, but she saw how close to breaking I was as things were unraveling. We bit the financial bullet, hoping that I was older and wiser because of what happened.

In case you are wondering, the police did their best, but as was explained to me, scammers could be in the next city or some distant country and are almost impossible to trace. One thing I can share is that throughout my time spent with a local detective, I never once felt disrespected, looked down on, or given a "You got what you deserve" attitude. For that, I am thankful.

Thoughts from Registrants

I asked readers of *Into the Light*,
"What have been your experiences dealing with the registry?"

Yes, I have the registry to keep up with, but it is what you make of it.

***

When I was homeless, I had to call in once every seven days and report where I was sleeping every night. I had to keep my GPS ankle bracelet charged at least once a day. If I didn't follow those rules, I could have ended up locked up.

***

I have no problems dealing with the registry.

***

Registration was simple and only took about 15 minutes. The attitude of the parolee makes a difference in how they will be treated when registering. I kept remembering that they were only doing their job, and I put myself in their position. Being transparent goes a long way. It gains the respect of others and makes a person feel good.

***

If you can get or afford to have representation, do it. There are professionals who can ease the process and guide you to what you should expect is right. Some administrators set registry levels (usually 1, 2, or 3) in a way that makes registration more difficult because of being too strict. An attorney will fight for what is fair. Compliance can be easy if you are a 1. If you are a 2, it can be more awkward and difficult as far as meeting at the local police station, especially in terms of finding appointment times. However, be professional, humble, and friendly.

***

I had no problems directly with the registry. The records office here handles it, and the main lady who does everything is very kind and helpful with whatever questions you may have. She never judged me and wished only the best life for me.

***

The Registry requires me to report four times a year because I'm considered a Sexually Violent Predator (SVP). I think this is mostly just a title they use to punish us for crimes we have already served time for. I see it as a continual type of punishment for our crimes when no other crimes are treated like ours.

Part Eight
Successful Reentry In My Opinion

14

My Personal List

In the introduction to this book, I wrote that my intent was not to produce a resource guide for someone in reentry. I would not be offering transitional living addresses, no registrant-friendly employers, or churches. There would, however, be some information that might help.

Instead, I wanted to share experiences with you, especially how I felt about reentry and the problems I and others have faced. People will sometimes ask, "How are you doing?" and the temptation to say, "Fine," when things aren't fine will be very real. It takes a good deal of inner strength, however, to respond, "I'm having trouble finding a job (or a place to live or worship)" instead of saying, "Fine."

Sometimes, people will answer by offering you a connection that might solve your problem, but most times, it won't. They will walk away from the conversation knowing more about you, though. You haven't dismissed them with the easy answer of "Fine." You have given them something to think about. *You.*

Everyone has a personality that makes them unique. If that's the case (and it is), the things that are important to us, and maybe *why* they are important to us, are just as unique. Some of what I am about to share might have been seen in what you have already read, but maybe not. The only thing on my list that will always be at the top of my list is at the top of my list.

God is No.1 – always will be

One of the men who offered thoughts for this book emphasized the importance of having a higher power. The 12-step program used by Alcoholics Anonymous (AA) has as its second step "Came to believe that a Power greater than ourselves could restore us to sanity."

The wording is very important for AA because while the problem is alcohol and all who attend share an addiction to it, not everyone who attends a 12-step program believes in God.

The first step states, "We admitted we were powerless over alcohol - that our lives had become unmanageable." I have learned to substitute "sexual addiction" for "alcohol" and believe that we all could offer whatever drives us out of control as a substitute.

The 12-step programs identify the addictive problem as most important and then speak of a higher Power able to restore. You might feel I am just playing with words, but I reverse the steps.

Following my daily moral compass means that I recognize God as my heavenly Father, Jesus as my Redeemer, and the Holy Spirit as the presence of God existing within me. The Bible is both an introduction to the things of God and a road map for my spiritual journey.

Any choices I make in my life that go against that map are, in my opinion, a choice to move not toward God but away from Him. My faith, however, reminds me that God never turns from me and *never* stops loving me.

When I was a boy, I was taught that we all have a conscience, an inner voice that makes clear what is right and what is wrong. I wasn't always sure *why* something was wrong, but I never doubted the feeling that it *was*.

As a child, the wrongs I chose were little things – telling a fib, swiping an extra cookie when I thought no one was looking. But as I grew into manhood, my wrong choices got darker and deeply affected other people.

Eventually, the line I crossed harmed children who trusted me. Like the alcoholic, I knew I was sinking. I also knew I couldn't change. I believed that every time I sinned in this way, God had turned His back until I cried out, "Please, forgive me!"

[14] But each person is tempted when he is lured and enticed by his own desire. [15] Then desire when it has conceived gives birth to sin, and sin when it is fully grown brings forth death.

James 1:14-16 ESV

⁸ If we say we have no sin, we deceive ourselves, and the truth is not in us. ⁹ If we confess our sins, he is faithful and just to forgive us our sins and to cleanse us from all unrighteousness.

1 John 1:8-9

The first set of verses always frightened me because I believed my inability to stop molesting meant I was dead in the eyes of God. The second verse changed that fear, even though the words didn't mean all my issues would disappear or that all would be right with the world.

What they did mean was that if I kept my struggle a secret, it would always have control over me, but confessing my sins would, however, break that wall of secrecy.

In every story I could share with you about my own reentry, I can point to God's presence in everything that happened.

¹⁷ Every good gift and every perfect gift is from above, coming down from the Father of lights, with whom there is no variation or shadow due to change. (emphasis mine)

James 1:17 NABRE

The more I looked for God in my everyday reentry experiences, the more I recognized he was there. Sometimes I knew that from the start. Other times, I would say, "Only God could have made that happen!" Why would I choose anything else to head my list?

HONESTY IS ALWAYS THE BEST POLICY.

Molestation is always a betrayal of trust and an act shrouded in secrecy, the kind of secrecy that makes future abuse possible if not probable. The truth is that self-protecting lies occupied more space in me than the presence of truth when it came to dealing with my addiction.

Perhaps the greatest freedom I felt while still in prison was that truth became more important to me than how others might have felt about me, knowing some of my hidden secrets. For much of my adult life, I created an image of the man I wanted others to *think* I was. In becoming that image for the sake of others, I refused life to the man I was meant to be. I know. It can be confusing.

In reentry, honesty goes a long way, especially with people who know what you have done and where you spent the past years. You might remember the story I shared of the young man who enthusiastically claimed complete freedom from temptation, saying, "God has set me free!" Maybe he really believed that. Maybe what he shared with us was what he thought we wanted to hear.

> *31 So Jesus said to the Jews who had believed him, "If you abide in my word, you are truly my disciples, 32 and you will know the truth, and the truth will set you free."*

> John 8:31-32 ESV

When I am tempted to "shade the truth" to what I think is to my benefit, I remind myself that the truth always sets me free. Choosing the truth is not always easy, but it is the best option. And you know what? People seem to recognize a truthful person when they meet one. Jesus did.

> *Jesus saw Nathanael coming toward him and said of him, "Behold, an Israelite indeed, in whom there is no deceit!"*

> John 1:47 ESV

I try to tell the truth, not so that others will see me as a truthful man. I tell the truth because the truth does, indeed, set me free.

I can't change the past, but I can change.

"When I get out, everyone is going to know what I have done. They are going to make my life miserable, so what's the point of even trying to start over? Besides, I am who I am." (An inmate's letter)

My past with all its shame is a matter of public record for anyone who cares to take the time to look it up. Being human, I hope they don't, but it would be their choice, not mine to control.

I understand how writing a biography for treatment forces someone to confront what they have done – maybe for the first time – but I disagree with the idea of wearing that biography as a permanent identification. In my opinion, my biography is not "who I am" but "what I did." A biography is part of taking responsibility for my actions. It should not, however, be the goal of any treatment program. It should not define me for all time. "I am who I am" seems to be the words of someone who believes their biography defines who they are instead of what they did.

The reality, however, is that my first days out of prison were awkward, especially as I was returning to the same city where people knew me well. But it was equally awkward for others when they saw me.

As I entered a local store, I caught a glimpse of someone from the same church I attended. I turned away to avoid eye contact, but when I looked back, he was gone – until I saw him in one of the store's security mirrors, crouched over and headed to the exit.

One thing I have learned over the past 37 years is that "everyone" is not looking for an opportunity to do me harm. I am on the state's registry, but I doubt many people visit that website looking for information about me. If people have issues with me, they have not been shared with me face-to-face.

I don't believe that it is my responsibility to change the minds of others who consider me an active "sex offender." My responsibility is to do whatever it takes to become a better, more God-centered version of me. If others notice changes in me, that's great, but if they don't, I can't change that. Trying to do so would be a waste of energy and a source of frustration that I don't need.

Most people are familiar with the "Serenity Prayer," especially those involved in 12-step programs. Usually, however, it is only the first four lines that are quoted. Personally, I find as much strength, if not more, in the second half of the prayer.

THE SERENITY PRAYER

God grant me the serenity.
to accept the things I cannot change;
courage to change the things I can;
and wisdom to know the difference.
Living one day at a time;

enjoying one moment at a time;
accepting hardships as the pathway to peace;
taking, as he did, this sinful world
as it is, not as I would have it;
trusting that he will make all things right
if I surrender to his will;
that I may be reasonably happy in this life
and supremely happy with him
forever in the next.
Amen.
Reinhold Niebuhr (1892-1971)

BE PATIENT AND TRUST GOD.

Some institutions today try to help those nearing release with internal reentry programs, but the process can be very frustrating, especially for those who have completed long sentences.

It is not by accident that the title of this book is "New Life - New Directions." From my own experiences and from those in reentry who share, we all faced a different world when we walked out of prison. There were new buildings. Lots of them. Whole new residential and commercial developments had sprung up where once there had been farmland or empty fields.

Most of us had not driven a car for years, and our licenses had expired. In some cases, we also needed a birth certificate, a social security card, and a personal banking account. And the list goes on.

Technology, even for those who believe themselves to be tech-savvy, has moved more deeply into things like AI (artificial intelligence) or ChatGPT and has left some of us in the dust of their progress. Cell phones are no longer just phones, but devices built to do just about everything a computer does. Cellphones can also connect with the internet, something forbidden for many registrants.

Despite all the physical changes, reentry involves the basics: finding a job, a place to live, and support (whether a support group system or a faith community). For all those things to happen, reentry is also all about patience and trusting that things will come together.

I was hired for my first full-time job six years after my release.

Before that, I worked a series of part-time jobs – never making much more than what it took to cover our basic expenses. When I received my first check as a full-time employee, I called the human resources department to ask if a mistake had been made or if I would be paid monthly. "No mistake. The check you received is your two-week salary."

GIVE PEOPLE TIME

"What's with people? I spent years in prison, did everything I was told to do, reconnected in my relationship with God, but I feel rejected wherever I go – especially in church." (Inmate letter)

I felt that way myself, and sometimes sensing rejection made me angry. Worse than anger, however, was the desire to reject *them*. I knew that doing that meant isolating myself again, the same kind of isolation that put me at risk. Instead of turning my back on people, I looked for new ways to connect, but my unease with rejection was still a matter to resolve.

Understanding did eventually come, but I can't tell you whether I read what I am about to share or heard someone say it. The important thing is to tell you that it made all the difference.

When news of my arrest hit the paper, people struggled with how to feel about a man who seemed to be a good guy, a church and song leader, and a man most people liked. Their feelings fell into one of two categories: deep anger for what I had done, or "He couldn't have done that! Somebody has it wrong."

Most of my friends and relatives, as well as our rather large church family, avoided me during the year it took to go through the court system. The day I was sentenced, I think there was resolution for some because prison was to be my new home, and that was fine with them. For others who wondered if I was guilty, the argument didn't make much difference. I was in prison. I was no longer occupying the same space with them.

If I consider my sentencing date as Point A, I could also claim my release date as Point B. Much had happened between A and B, much good and much change.

On the other hand, for most other people, my Point B was seen as the day after Point A. In other words, deep feelings surfaced as people struggled with how they felt about my return.

I wanted everyone to be on the same page as me. I wanted them to acknowledge the treatment programs, my remorse, and my sincere desire to be reconciled with them in some way. But that's what I wanted, and that was not something in my control. Sometimes, even after so many years, when I still think it unfair that others refuse to see those changes or even acknowledge their possibility, God reminds me that my journey is still to follow him in all things. He will take care of everyone and everything else.

Thoughts from Registrants

I asked readers of *Into the Light*,
"Is there anything else that might be
helpful to registrants?"

Living right is going to make things easier, and the easiest way to do that is to find a big church and follow God's word. This is going to give you encouragement. It's going to lift you up. You may feel convicted sometimes by the message because of your past sins, but God will deliver you out of your feeling of conviction, because his love overcomes and does not end. And when you follow his way and invest your time in him (church, Bible study, volunteer groups), people will see you are for real. You have changed. You do right. You are new.

***

Be calm and patient. Not everyone everywhere will be the same. Every state is not the same, nor will all parolees have the same stipulations. Some of us will have to register for life, some will not. Some of us have had treatment on the inside, so outside counseling is easier. Some will face a challenge of confronting issues we have never dealt with or even had a chance to do so.

I have found honesty to be a true respecter; be honest with those you get close to, as if they want to invest in you and your success. They will want the truth.

I was completely honest with a lady who is a co-worker and has become my No. 1 support person and my good friend. She does not approve of what I did, but has allowed me to prove I want to change. She has stood by me and continues to help me grow and set goals.

***

Don't make mountains out of molehills. Be patient because things will eventually work out. Always remember that no matter how many rules or restrictions, it beats being in prison. To disobey or ignore the rules is a fast ticket back. So, follow the rules, pray for strength, and be patient.

***

If you want to stay out of trouble, you will do what you can to keep going in the right direction. You will be much happier if you do, as will your family and friends.

***

Looking back, those were dark days when I self-reported that I was molesting a family member. Giving a 141-page confession to five detectives was a painful experience. I knew I needed help and believed they were going to be there for me. But their job was to get an eventual conviction. There was no sympathy to be found.

In my state, a person being incarcerated will be strip-searched, showered, and donned with an orange jumpsuit. Being naked and told to squat had its own degree of shame and humiliation. I did not sleep much at all that night after being handcuffed and put in a holding cell with a dozen others.

Being put in a cell the next morning was better than the time in the holding cell. Transfer to the new cell already had two guys in it on the bunk beds, so I ended up sleeping on the concrete floor.

Sleeping an hour or so, I was told by a guard that I was being released. Thankfully, after three days or so, my wife was able to secure my bail. I was threatened with divorce if this ever happened again.

The road to recovery and healing for our family had just begun. Disclosing my actions was, at the same time, breaking a shame and secrecy cycle that I did not want to take to the grave. Another intent was to give the victim a fighting chance at recovery.

***

One problem is having to wear a GPS bracelet, but I don't mention it to people and keep it covered up. I do have problems with the bracelet, but the monitoring center is good about contacting me or me contacting them about any problems. They send out a service agent to correct the problem by replacing the bracelet.

***

You can make it in the world, though I am glad I went through treatment, even though I don't agree with how it is administered after I served my time. But it was still beneficial and has helped me daily.

I'm still involved with ministries that supported me through my incarceration. One has an "Our Daily Bread" conference seven days a week. We are a family and have a Zoom bible study on Mondays.

If you are reading this book and are locked up, don't give up hope. Reach out to ministries and healthy alternatives. My higher power is Jesus Christ, and I encourage all of you to have a higher power.

I am coming to the end of *New Life - New Directions* but want to share one more offering from a man in reentry. What he wrote was a testimony that speaks truth, sometimes difficult truth. Every day is a challenge and a blessing. A challenge because some of the darkness shows itself, yet a blessing because if we are willing, God's grace will give us victory.

There can be no more victims. Just remember, God doesn't call you "child molester." He calls you by your name. And he loves you!

"Call on God . . .He Will Answer"

A Testimony (1999)

At the age of two or three, my siblings and I were taught to be sexual with each other by an adult cousin who was babysitting. At the age of four, my oldest brother began to abuse me, and the sexual encounters lasted until shortly before his marriage.

Since I have spent my entire life being sexually active, my mind and body separated from God. Many times, I called out for God's help and sometimes had brief periods of His saving grace. In the end, however, I would choose the things of the world I craved (including molesting children) and turn my back on God. I would choose the things that gave me control and, because of my choices, became estranged from God and people, making a cocoon for myself out of the lies of lust.

I wanted out but could not pull away. Parks, bookstores, gay bars, drugs, and alcohol were each followed by times when I attended church, AA meetings, and retreats. I would fall on my knees pleading for God to help me, but when I got up, I would do the same things all over again.

My life was in turmoil. Getting married and still living a double life. Fathering children but not knowing how to be a father. Finally, molesting another child and being found out. What I felt was the shame, the burden, the fear, and the unending stream of tears as I cried to God for help.

I told lies so that I wouldn't really have to talk about my sins. The institution gave me medication daily, and I attended church and

AA meetings again. My wife had decided to stay with me during this time. My children loved me despite my crimes, but when it was time for me to go home, the state said I couldn't because the children would be there. Once more, I cried to God for help, and He placed me in a Christian halfway house close to home. My heart sang out that God was real … my heart told me that I must seek Him.

One day, an accusation was made that I molested another child. Family members were divided. After all, why should they have believed me? Yet again, I called on God for help and, because of His grace, made it through that period.

One year from my out date, permission was granted for me to go home to my family, but there was no home to go to. My mother-in-law had asked my wife and three children to leave her house. God directed us to a Christian church campground where we lived in a tent for months. As a response to our ongoing prayers, God provided a house for us. I had no job at the time and was a sex offender. Only God could have brought this about.

To buy the house, however, I needed a better job–one with benefits. Every evening, our family held hands and prayed, trusting the Lord to provide for our needs. And He did. I now have a job.

One afternoon, while grocery shopping with my wife, I found myself face-to-face with my last victim. I left my wife there and went to the car, but the young man followed. Once outside, he released the rage he felt toward me by shouting to everyone who would listen that I was a molester and that I had molested him.

The man I had become was not a molester, but the man I had been was. I knew that God had been changing my life and encouraging new choices, but I still felt torn by the hate voiced in my direction. I got in the car and drove off, returning later to pick up my wife. I called my agent and reported the incident as best I could, and was told I had done the right thing.

A change *has* taken place. God has done for me what I could not do for myself. He has picked me up and set me on the path to Him and let me know that He will *always* be there for me. I still fail him, but I know that I don't want to. I only wish to honor God for He sent His Son to love me and atone for my sins. His love is felt with every breath I take.

Epilogue

I am so thankful for those in reentry who share their progress with me, because I know some of the challenges registrants face. Each day is a new life we get to experience, a life where we decide which direction we choose to take. It's not always easy, but that's true for everyone.

When I first considered writing this book, I knew it would not be a one-size-fits-all collection of steps to take, nor would I be able to offer a plan that would guarantee reentry success. But I do remember the hours I spent years ago wondering what reentry would be like for me. I asked myself a lot of questions without getting answers.

I knew, however, that once I was finally starting life over, my expectations had to include the possibility that others might already have decided who I was and/or whether I could be trusted. I also knew that not everyone would want me back among them.

I had been "away," living in an environment I didn't think I could explain even if someone asked – and no one did, though I often wished they might want to know.

But I also remember a man I met in the county jail who told me where I would be sent once the state evaluated me based on my offenses and my sentence structure. He described the buildings I would see and how some aspects of prison life worked at that facility. Best of all, he gave me simple yet invaluable advice that I soon recognized as a way not only to survive but grow. He was right on all accounts, and I thank God for introducing the two of us.

Remembering all those things, *New Life - New Directions* was written for those wanting help navigating reentry, not as a how-to book, but as perhaps a measuring stick to help them deal with their own moments of uncertainty. God willing, readers will find something that helps and encourages them. And maybe, I hope, they will be able to pass on what helped them to someone else looking for that same kind of help.

The following verses have sustained me many times over the years, and I hope that they will serve you as well.

> *¹I waited patiently for the Lord;*
> *he turned to me and heard my cry.*
> *² He lifted me out of the slimy pit,*
> *out of the mud and mire;*
> *he set my feet on a rock*
> *and gave me a firm place to stand.*
> *³ He put a new song in my mouth,*
> *a hymn of praise to our God.*
> *Many will see and fear the Lord*
> *and put their trust in him.*
>
> Psalm 40:1-3 NIV

If you take nothing else from this book, believe this:

YOU ARE A CHILD OF GOD!

<u>Booklets written by Bob Van Domelen:</u>

Prison and Homosexuality

When Darkness Isn't Dark Enough: A Discussion

The Church, Sex Offenders, and Reconciliation

<u>Newsletter written by Bob Van Domelen</u>
Into the Light
(support for registrants)
Published bi-monthly – *no third-party requests*
Newsletter is available by writing

Broken Yoke Ministries
PO Box 5824
De Pere, WI 54115-5824

Website
https:// brokenyoke.org
Email
Bob@brokenyoke.org

Acknowledgments

Many thanks to friends who have blessed my life with their support and encouragement. Being able to walk into a room and feel welcome is not something I take for granted. Special thanks to my wife, who supports me, loves me, and prays for me. Divorce is common and even expected by registrants, so having her at my side is also never something I take for granted. Special thanks to Karen Hart (KEYS Ministry) for sending out questionnaires to registrants in reentry used in the "In Our Opinion" offerings. Her support and prayers have been a blessing for years. Thanks, also, to those in reentry who responded to my request for their opinion.